NEW ENGLAND BIRD LOVER'S GARDEN

Attracting Birds with Plants and Flowers

Randi Minetor
Photographs by Nic Minetor

Globe
Pequot

Guilford, Connecticut

Globe
Pequot

An imprint of Rowman & Littlefield
Distributed by NATIONAL BOOK NETWORK

Copyright © 2016 by Rowman & Littlefield
All photography by Nic Minetor

British Library Cataloguing in Publication Information Available

Library of Congress Cataloging-in-Publication Data is available on file.

ISBN 978-1-4930-2234-2 (paperback)
ISBN 978-1-4930-2235-9 (e-book)

∞™ The paper used in this publication meets the minimum requirements of American National Standard for Information Sciences—Permanence of Paper for Printed Library Materials, ANSI/NISO Z39.48-1992.

Contents

Northern mockingbird

Introduction

Why do more than sixty-eight million people in America watch birds? Perhaps it's the birds' seemingly infinite diversity in limitless combinations—the remarkable variety of sizes, colors, songs, and behavior patterns we can observe. Once we look beyond the sooty pigeons at the bus station or the starlings soaring in synchronized flocks over congested highways, the diversity of this family of the animal kingdom is staggering. In North America alone, we can count more than 950 bird species that either breed in the continental United States and Canada, or put in regular appearances around the continent's fringes as they drift over from faraway shores.

Birds telegraph the change of seasons, they clear last year's berries off of your bushes and reduce the number of grubs in your lawn, and they brighten your mornings with their song. They already share your garden and your neighborhood with you, but perhaps you haven't formally invited them over for dinner. This book tells you how to extend that invitation, by planting the right flowers, shrubs and trees and putting out the right foods and drinks to make your garden their favorite place to dine.

Dedicated garden birders in New England can tell you that over the course of a year, you might see more than seventy different species in your own yard—from hawks, geese, and gulls passing overhead to many varieties of sparrows, finches, and other small birds at your feeders and in your shrubs and trees. If you're fortunate enough to live on the edge of a pond or lake, in a farming community, or near a desert—or if you have a large property with many trees—your backyard visitors may expand to number more than one hundred different species.

Whether your backyard is a compact square in a subdivision, an expansive suburban lawn, a mowed oasis surrounded by open land or forest, or a windswept landing on a bluff overlooking the ocean, you can bring birds into your yard to enjoy their life cycle of courtship, nesting, raising young, and departing for warmer climates. You needn't be a master gardener or a top-notch birder to engage with the feathered creatures in your area—in fact, all you need to do is follow a twentieth-century song lyric: "Find out what they like and how they like it, and let 'em have it just that way."

Many a beginning bird gardener can point to experiments that failed and plants that perished—but you don't have to suffer through such wallet-draining mistakes. This book will help you make the right choices the first time, whether it's the purchase of shrubs that will fill your yard with berry-eating birds all winter, or selection of the most effective oriole feeder and what to put in it to bring bright orange birds to your window.

We offer many recommendations for plants that actively attract birds—some for the seeds they produce when the flowers fade, and others for their wealth of fruit, dense foliage that provides cover, and strong limbs that serve as stable nesting locations. As you plan your own garden or transform your existing landscape with native species, we urge you to consult your local nursery to find the hardiest species for your habitat. What works on the Atlantic coast may not thrive in the mountains of Vermont and New Hampshire, so choose your plants wisely for your own landscape.

By following the principles in this book, you can turn your yard into the habitat of choice for all manner of marvelous birds.

House finch on seed feeder
near branch clamped to porch

1 Bird Lover's Garden Essentials

Before you begin choosing feeders, buying bags of bird food and planting flowers that will produce seeds and nectar, make sure you're ready to enjoy the birds that will most certainly arrive in your yard.

Just as the birds need food, water, and shelter, you need a few essentials to make your bird lover's garden experience as rich and colorful as it can be. Let's start with the birding basics, so the garden you create will bring you the most enjoyable birding experience.

A CLEAR VIEW

Where in your house can you sit comfortably and look out a window? Whether you have a wide bay window in your dining room, a sliding glass door off of your kitchen, or a portal near your desk in your home office, you'll want to place the plants that will attract birds where they can be seen from that window. This is particularly important when wintry weather can keep you from spending a lot of time on a deck, porch, or patio. Looking out the window over your morning coffee and watching a variety of birds feasting at your feeders or in your shrubs can make a frigid, overcast winter day seem a great deal brighter.

You don't need a panoramic, ceiling-to-floor window to enjoy the view of birds visiting your yard. Choose the window that reveals the greatest number of natural features—trees, shrubs, water (puddles count!), and lower plants. Be sure to select comfortable furniture for your viewing window. You may find yourself sitting for extended periods, so have a well-padded chair, a table on which to take notes, and quick access to food and drink. It's no wonder that most people choose their kitchen table to serve as Bird Watching Central.

We often look out windows without really seeing what is there: overgrown shrubs that block the view, vines that crisscross the glass, or old and dirt-clogged screens that obscure what lies beyond. What features of your yard can you see? Are there trees and shrubs that could provide places to hang viewable feeders? Where might you add a birdbath or brush pile that might attract birds within your line of sight? Where could you plant a flowering tree or shrub that will produce berries to attract a wider variety of birds?

Remember, nothing brightens a room or improves a view more than a clean window. Wash your windows with warm water and mild soap at least twice a year, using a soft cloth or an old T-shirt. Use a squeegee to help minimize the potential for streaking. If you've got stubborn stains or embedded soils, many professionals swear by a solution of two parts distilled white vinegar and one part water. This will remove hard water spots, dirt, and other gunk, without generating harmful ammonia fumes.

However, beware of dangers that clean windows will pose to the birds outside. Birds may see only the reflections of trees, sky, and clouds and fly headlong into the glass. Experts say that millions of birds are killed by window strikes each year. You can help by adding one or more warning decals that let birds know something solid is ahead. The best ones absorb ultraviolet light, so they are translucent to humans, but bright blue to birds.

A FIELD GUIDE

You may think at first that a field guide is only for serious birders who get up at dawn to catch glimpses of unusual species. The first time a bird you don't recognize lands at one of your feeders, however, you will wish for a quick reference book to tell you what kind of bird has arrived in your yard.

How do you choose the right guide for you? First, look for a book that has "Field Guide" in its title. Many books offer photos or illustrations of birds, but only the field guides are fully comprehensive. Dozens of reference books are available to help you determine what birds you see. Many field guides cover the entire bird population of the eastern or western half of the United States, with the Mississippi River as the rough dividing line. Others focus on one bird family, such as warblers, sparrows, hummingbirds, or shorebirds. Even if you believe that you will never see anything more unusual than house sparrows and juncos in your backyard, you will very likely be pleasantly surprised by the wide variety.

OPTICS

You need binoculars.

Even if you only watch the birds in your own backyard, the day will come when a bird will land in a distant

CHOOSING A FIELD GUIDE

Should you use a guide with photos or illustrations? Try both kinds of guides to determine which you prefer. Photo guides provide single, vivid examples of each bird, usually in breeding plumage. Illustrated guides provide many drawings of the same species. These guides give you an idea of all the possible plumage variations, revealing fine shades of identification. Many bird lovers have one of each kind to improve their ability to identify an unexpected species—or to recognize a bird that looks like a familiar species, but may be in juvenile or winter plumage.

Go to your local bookstore or birders' specialty store and browse through the titles. Look at the size and weight of the guides, and think about where you will keep this guide in your house. Do you want a guide that will fit in a coat pocket, or one that offers larger type and illustrations on a bigger page?

The best field guides provide many different views of the same bird species, so you can see the differences between the male and female birds of the same species. Other views show you how the bird might change in winter, or how an immature bird might look. There's a map on each page as well. Map colors tell you where the bird lives in each season: summer, winter, or year-round, and its migratory path.

Try a number of field guides to decide which works best for you.

Don't feel that you must restrict yourself to one choice. Many experienced birders keep a copy of every field guide on the market along with their binoculars. The ability to compare different photos and illustrations can help you sharpen your identification skills, while giving you enough information about a bird's size, markings, and behavior to make a well-informed decision about the bird's species.

When a brightly colored migrant bird shows up unexpectedly in the shrubs near your viewing window, you don't want to have to scramble for your field guide. Keep your field guide and binoculars close to your viewing window. If you have more than one viewpoint, consider having a field guide and binoculars at each place. Have a notebook and pen or pencil handy as well, to take notes about the bird's markings and activity before you look for it in the field guide.

tree, and you'll want a closer look at an unfamiliar wing pattern or unusual breast color. Binoculars open up the world of birds to the casual viewer in a way that no other tool can.

But which pair is right for you? Here are the most important things to understand about the way binoculars work:

You'll see what looks like a size or formula, usually stamped on the focus knob. It may say 7 x 35, 8 x 50, or 10 x 40, or another combination of numbers.

The first number is the number of times the binoculars magnify the image of the bird for you. If the first number is 7, for example, the binoculars show you the bird at 7 times its normal size.

So you may think that a magnification of 10 would be the best, right? The fact is that 10x binoculars can be very hard to hold still enough to see a clear image at 10 times its normal size. Unless you're using the binoculars exclusively on a tripod, the 10x pair will probably frustrate you more than thrill you. Most birders prefer a pair with 7x or 8x magnification.

The second number (35, 40, 42, or 50) is a measurement of the amount of light that comes through the large end of the binoculars. It's actually the diameter of the objective (larger) lens, in millimeters. Here larger is better, as it allows you to see more clearly in low light situations—near dusk or on overcast days.

Ask your retailer about the binoculars' field of view. A wider field of view is better for spotting a bird, as you have more area that you can see—giving you a greater opportunity to find the bird in your lens.

Finally, look for optics that are fully multi-coated. This is critically important, as binoculars with full, multiple coatings will reduce color fringing (the blue or yellow halo around the image), producing a clear, crisp view of the bird. A sharp image is the result of many different coatings on each lens. Just about all of today's binoculars have some coatings. Some very reasonably priced optics are

You should be able to hold binoculars comfortably in one hand.

fully multi-coated, which means that every piece of glass inside the binoculars—as many as eighteen surfaces—has multiple coatings. Each layer reduces the reflective scattering of light between these glass surfaces, eliminating glare and distortion. Coated optics look dark and often greenish or bluish when you look at the objective lens.

The right price

The top binoculars may run as much as $1,500 per pair—which is extreme for looking at birds in your own yard. Don't feel that you must purchase the absolute best. Instead, buy the best you can afford. If you are new to birding, you may want to begin with a modest pair. You might choose a smaller-diameter objective lens or a lower magnification, but don't skimp on the coatings! Spending $125 instead of $50 will make an enormous difference in your enjoyment.

SPOTTING SCOPES

If you're just getting started with watching birds and you have a fairly standard city or suburban yard, a spotting scope may not be a high priority. But if your property backs up to a pond or lake, a big open field, or a wetland, or if your neighbors have large trees or shrubs that attract birds, a scope will bring many out-of-reach birds into sharp focus.

Birds have a frustrating tendency to hide just beyond your ability to see them. A scope can help extend your viewing range, sometimes by hundreds of feet, so you can see the scarlet tanager in your neighbor's oak or the Baltimore oriole at the feeder across the street.

Just as binoculars come in many shapes and sizes, scopes run the gamut of varieties as well. A visit to your favorite birders' specialty store or outdoor outfitter will

Spotting scopes come in many sizes and price points.

reveal the wide range of spotting scopes available. As you will see, a good scope is a fairly major investment.

Scopes generally begin at 20x, magnifying the bird 20 times for your enjoyment. On some models, you can choose an eyepiece that zooms in to an astonishing 50x or 60x, making birds look so close, they could be sitting on your hand. Look for fully multi-coated optics, which will decrease distortion, increase the contrast of the image, and give you a sharp, clear, and vibrant view of the bird. Get the largest objective (front) lens you can afford. A 60 or 65mm lens is excellent; an 80mm lens will let in much more light and deliver a brighter image.

There's more to a scope purchase than the scope itself: Your scope is only as good as the tripod that holds it upright. You need a tripod that will hold steady while you look through the lens, even if you're outside on a windy day. A tripod that vibrates or sways will make it very difficult to get a clear view of the bird.

KEEP A YARD LIST

It's fun to keep a list of every bird you see in and around your yard. Whether you start writing down the bird species you see to track them from day to day, month to month, or as a year-to-year comparison record, keeping a yard list will become your passion in no time.

Start by jotting down the bird species you see. Keep a pad and pen by the window from which you watch your feeders. Write down what you see that day, during that week, or month. Make additional notes if you see bird behavior that strikes you as interesting. If a bird arrives in unusual plumage, note this as well. Soon you will have a

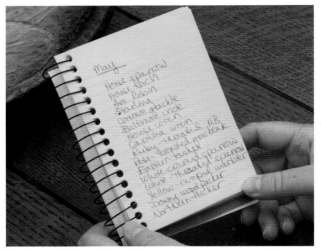

May
House Sparrow
House Finch
Am. Robin
Starling
Common grackle
Baltimore oriole
House wren
Carolina wren
Ruby-throated H.B.
Rose-breasted grosbeak
Eastern towhee
White-crowned sparrow
White-throated sparrow
Yellow-rumped warbler
Downy woodpecker
Northern flicker

Keeping a yard list can be fun and easy.

sense of which birds arrive in various seasons, and which are with you year-round.

Once you have a list established, watching your bird garden provides a wonderful opportunity to enjoy the natural change of seasons. You might begin writing down all the birds you see each month, starting a new page on the first of the month, and recording the dates on which you add species to the month list. As you see bird species for the first time during the year, you will know that the migration has begun—often before any significant change in the weather occurs.

By comparing one year's list to the next, you can know when it's time to put out your hummingbird and oriole feeders, or when the woodpeckers and nuthatches will need the extra protein in raw suet.

GO MOBILE

Do you want to keep your bird list with you wherever you go? There's an app for that, of course. In fact, there are a number of options, with color pictures of each bird species, information about their migration patterns and residency, and even recordings of their songs. Having your bird list on your mobile phone can help you increase the number of birds on your life list, while providing an instant field guide when something new flies into view.

Masses of flowers and shrubs create a natural habitat for birds.

2 Create a Garden Bird Paradise

If you were a bird, where would you live: a carefully mani-cured lawn with exquisitely clipped topiary and sparse plant-ings of exotic flowers, or a lush carpet of native wildflowers edged with dense, leafy shrubs and berry-laden trees?

If you chose the latter garden, you've already learned something about your feathered guests. Birds need food, water, and shelter, the three factors that a natural garden can provide with ease. While professionally maintained, sculpted gardens may delight the eyes of many gardeners, they're often turn-offs for native birds.

Planning a garden for the birds begins with an understanding of what birds need, your property's exist-ing elements, and the plants that are native to your area. (Consult Appendix B: Northeast Hardiness Zone Map on page 208 to determine your hardiness zone.)

PLANNING YOUR BIRD LOVER'S GARDEN

Begin your garden planning process by drawing a sketch of your yard and existing plantings. Use your favorite drafting or garden planning software if you wish, but a piece of graph paper and some colored pencils will do the trick as well.

Measure your property so your drawing will be as true to scale as possible. You don't need special skills for this; simply decide that each square of the graph paper represents one square foot. If that will make the drawing too large, each square can represent two or three feet, or whatever makes sense for your garden space.

Once you have the border on paper, add the existing trees, shrubs, and flower beds. Now you can see the spaces between what's already there.

It's common practice in American gardening to plant single, freestanding perennial flowers, as well as shrubs and trees. Layers of mulch often extend between them, creating carefully groomed areas in which the individual plantings stand out. This may make a garden neat and orderly, but such a layout does not help you attract birds.

Instead, look at these blank spaces and consider how you can fill them. Create a garden in the natural style, one that will look like home to birds in your area. Instead of placing one shrub on its own, bring several shrubs of the same species together to create dense foliage and more effective shelter for birds. Lines of shrubs serve a purpose on the edges of your yard, where they help define your space—but an irregular grouping will seem more inviting to birds in your area. Planting shrubs in a group can also boost the pollination process. Shrubs like viburnum, American holly, and blueberries produce more fruit when several shrubs are grouped together.

The trees and shrubs already in your yard provide a good starting point. Your next step will be to plant around these established features, making them part of a greater design.

Your natural garden will feature plants in masses, rather than two or three plants in a small clump. Each area will feature many varieties of perennials and some annuals as you choose, arranging short and tall plants to maximize the show in each season. Most important, the masses overlap, with no breaks between plant varieties.

If you have trees that provide a shape and foundation to your yard, begin to create a leafy understory beneath them with an assortment of low-growing and shade-loving plants. Many bloom with the first touch of spring, while others come into their peaks later in the summer, providing a continuous series of blossoms throughout the growing season.

In addition to floral beauty, the understory provides something important to ground-feeding birds: a safe, sheltered area under which they can forage for insects and invertebrates (like worms and grubs). You'll hear sparrows, thrushes, ground-feeding warblers, and other small birds rustling under the leaves as they search for morsels. If you like rabbits, this is a good way to attract them as well.

Ground covers and vines make excellent alternatives to grass, providing continuous color—often evergreen through the winter months—and a virtually maintenance-free lawn. Requiring a regular trimming around the edges to keep these vines in the territory of your choosing, native ground covers grow quickly and fill in bare landscapes, remaining hardy for many years.

In some regions, it's entirely acceptable to have no ground cover at all. Landscapes in drier areas may use gravel, crushed stone, or another rock or mineral option,

Dense plantings will pollinate easily, producing lots of blooms that attract birds.

eliminating the struggle with grass altogether. Such a yard can be planted with native shrubs that thrive in sandy soil or drought conditions, filling in the visual gaps while providing plenty of nesting habitat for wrens, towhees, and other birds that nest close to the ground.

Go native

One yard's weed is another yard's native flower, whether it's a daisy, an aster, a cluster of wild columbine or a naturalized daylily. You may wander through your local garden center and marvel at the number of Asian or African species it stocks each spring, but only a few of these exotic blooms will bring the birds into your yard. Generally, birds of New England will look for plants that are native to the region, the ones that have supplied these bird species with food sources long before humans started hanging feeders in their yards. It's the native plants that birds will turn to for nutrition, whether they feed on their seeds and fruit in late summer or drink the nectar they produce from spring to fall.

Look around at your garden as it stands today. What flowers do you see? You may already have some native species well established and thriving in your yard, because these flowers are the most suited to your climate, soil, and the insects and birds that are vital to their successful reproduction.

Make the most of these native flowers as you begin to choose new plants to expand your bird garden. Maybe it's time to add larger numbers of these established plants, creating masses of seed-producing blossoms that will feed your birds throughout the winter.

The flower species pictured in the next chapter are just a few of the hundreds of native blooms that may be right for your garden. These are some of the most popular flowers, well loved by gardeners for their dependable growth and ability to naturalize over time. They also deliver what birds need: nectar in spring or summer, and seeds in fall that can last throughout the winter.

Birds arriving during the spring migration will begin looking for food sources as they rest and refuel before continuing north. Seed heads from the previous year's native plants become a valuable source of nutrition, bringing varietal sparrows like fox, Lincoln's, and white-crowned into yards with large areas of plant life. Your wide bed of coneflower and black-eyed Susan can become a flock's dining room, helping them gather sustenance before they move farther north. As spring and summer blooms arrive, they will feed your resident sparrows, chickadees, titmice and other seedeaters.

Urban habitats

If you live in a dense residential area, or if the habitat around you suits people far better than it does birds, you can still make the most of your available space by creating a tiny oasis in the heart of the city.

You may not draw the wide range of colorful birds you would find in a wooded area or in a rural setting, but the birds you attract can be just as interesting to observe.

Birds of every species have complex social hierarchies, fascinating nesting and breeding cycles, and instinctive practices for teaching their young to fly, eat, and forage for food. Whether you have a small balcony on an upper floor or a townhouse with a sliding glass door that leads to a tiny patio, you can turn your limited space into a regular stop on your neighborhood birds' feeding rounds.

Your visitors may be slim and similar at first, especially if your proffered feeding site is at ground level on a city street. Over time, however, as birds passing overhead spot the activity below, you may attract common species beyond those most adapted to metro life. Any feeder in any city or suburb in North America will attract house sparrows, the continent's most common bird, and house finches often feed at the same feeders, even in the middle of cities. These birds have learned to share their territories with humans almost as effectively as the more aggressive house sparrows. These two species often compete for food, with the sparrows winning more rounds because of their slightly larger size and significantly greater numbers.

You are also likely to see European starlings and grackles as well. European starlings are often mistaken for "baby" grackles or blackbirds by beginning birders. Starlings are a separate species, with iridescent feathers in summer, and they're smaller and shorter-tailed than grackles. Large, long-tailed, bold, and noisy, grackles dominate starlings and most other birds at feeders—and they are comfortable perching on the feeder itself, while starlings generally feed on the ground.

As any city dweller has come to learn, the rock pigeon is highly adapted to cohabitation with humans in congested areas. They're just as happy eating from your trash or your takeout as they are with bird food, but the good news is you can depend on them to clean up the cheaper seed blends that other birds reject. Pigeons have unusually varied plumage within the species, and they've adapted their natural nesting behavior from cliff faces to ledges on high buildings. They may turn out to be more interesting than you think.

Before you create a downtown feeding station, however, find out if there's a peregrine falcon breeding project in your city. Some municipalities have embraced peregrines as residents because they eat rock pigeons. Peregrines often nest in boxes on tall buildings in city centers. If you'd rather not turn pigeons on your patio into sitting ducks for hunting peregrines, don't hang out feeders.

Wherever you live, the same basic principles for attracting birds apply: Birds need food, water, shelter, and places to nest. Provide as many of these as you can in your small space, and you can turn a stoop, porch, or slab into a compelling urban habitat.

Small-space garden

If you have a city house, townhouse or condominium with a small yard, you can create an inviting habitat by following just a few simple guidelines.

Create a sense of safety for birds by using border plants to define and enclose your space. For small lawns, build multidimensional borders with tall shrubs on the outside edge, and smaller shrubs and ground covers planted in close groups.

Add masses of perennial flowers that stand up to traffic, pets, and urban animal intrusion. Black-eyed Susans, daisies, sunflowers, and coneflowers are all resilient in urban gardens, while providing seeds the birds can eat in fall and winter.

Minimize the use of annual flowers planted on the ground, to keep them from being trampled in highly trafficked yard areas. Instead, plant flowers in sturdy pots, raising some on plant stands or pedestals to create the effect of several levels.

Hang flowering plants in pots along your fence, on brackets on your house's walls, or from porch or deck railings for birds flying over to see the colors that attract their attention. Baskets can hang near feeders—especially hummingbird feeders—to offer more than one source of food and nectar to passing birds.

Satisfy birds' need for shelter in your small space with shrubs that define their space. Even ground-feeding birds will find places to hide in shrubs along the ground, while taller shrubs enclose the space and provide a sense of security. Choose shrubs for their color as well as their height to create a dramatic visual effect as well. Finally, add a source of clean water to give birds even more reason to visit.

Find a spot for a small water feature: A freestanding birdbath with a water circulator will attract birds' attention. If you have just a little more room and access to an outdoor electrical outlet, a small man-made fountain with moving water will bring the small birds in your area to this clean, attractive water source.

City gardens can attract birds with water, shelter, and food.

Finally, add the feeders. Hang them from brackets off of a fence, from a deck railing, or from shepherd's crooks anchored in the ground in the midst of your plantings. Fill them with seeds or suet to attract the

Blue jay on a shelf (platform) feeder in a small-space garden

birds you hope will arrive—cardinals, finches, sparrows, thrushes, and others that may be in the area. Depend on the house sparrows, starlings, and pigeons to clean up the ground, an activity that other birds will spot and stop to investigate.

City dwellings may have fewer large windows than big suburban homes, so placing feeders where you can see them becomes a tricky process. Your deck, patio, or porch can offer an easy solution. All kinds of hanging apparatuses are available to attach to a railing or post. These hangers extend your feeder out beyond the deck or porch, so the seeds (and whatever else birds drop) fall to the ground instead of on your floor.

Container gardening

Apartment dwellers may have no ground to break for a garden, but you can still enjoy the pleasures of live plants and the birds that visit them.

Your patio or deck can become a mini-haven with the addition of plants in containers—not exotic houseplants, but the same plants you would place in a backyard.

Containers allow you to choose from a wide range of annuals and perennials, changing your garden every year as you learn which plants attract birds to your feeders. They also give you the flexibility to rearrange the setting—trying different levels, moving plants into or out of spots that get morning or afternoon sun, or placing whatever's in bloom closest to your feeders.

Garden centers, home improvement stores, and all kinds of pottery studios and boutiques offer ceramic and terra cotta pots that will hold up well against spring and

Containers bring flowers to a patio or porch.

summer's elements. Half the fun is finding the pots—they're as much of an expression of your creative spirit as are the shrubs and flowers you plant in them.

Consider half-barrels for shrubs, vines, and berry-producing plants like strawberry, blueberry, and raspberry—fruits you can share with your birds and you can enjoy as well. These larger containers may accommodate more than one plant, allowing you to create dynamic arrangements with plants and shrubs of different heights and colors.

Look for dwarf conifers and shrubs that remain small when fully grown. This is particularly important when creating a balcony garden, as plants that are too heavy may exceed the weight limit of your structure.

According to the American Conifer Society, dwarf conifers grow from 1 to 6 inches each year, topping out at no more than 6 feet in ten to fifteen years. You can choose from hundreds of varieties, many of which bear cones or berries that can help you attract birds to your container garden. Be sure to choose varieties that thrive in your climate and in the amount of sun and precipitation your patio receives.

Small tables and pedestals help create levels for your plants, either around the edges or grouped together in the corners of your deck or patio. The great thing about plants in pots is that you can arrange and rearrange them until you find the grouping that delights you. Adding a small table, a couple of plant stands, or a pedestal can help create a central element around which you can build a striking arrangement of colors, sizes, shrubs, and flowers. Finish the effect with cascading plants hanging from hooks overhead—and finally, add your feeders.

APARTMENT GARDEN RULES

Many landlords and rental properties have specific rules about the kinds of plants and other items you can have on your patio or deck. Before you begin a container garden, read your lease carefully to be sure your plans fit within its terms. If the lease isn't clear on this point, check with your landlord or building manager before proceeding.

Balcony gardening

If your apartment has a balcony, it's fun and easy to create a garden that will attract birds—as long as you're still fairly close to the ground.

Your second, third, or fourth floor balcony is still within most birds' feeding frame of reference. At the height of most suburban treetops, a balcony 30 feet above the ground provides a wonderful viewpoint from which to see birds in the tops of neighboring trees—eliminating the painful "warbler neck" birders get when they try to view high-perching birds from the ground with binoculars.

Hanging baskets, small containers and plants on pedestals help attract birds to a balcony.

Sparrows, cardinals, jays, warblers, flickers, and many other birds routinely fly and rest at these heights—but they may not be accustomed to finding food at 30 or 40 feet above the ground. It may take some time to attract birds to a new mini-habitat on your balcony, but you can be very successful in bringing the birds you'd like to see right up to your window.

If your balcony has a roof, birds may seek shelter under it during a rainstorm or on a windy day. Bird feeders and plants hung from roof supports can attract all manner of species, some of which may even nest in your hanging plant pot or on a shelf under the roof. Phoebes, robins, swallows, and pigeons all choose ledges and platforms in sheltered spots for their nests. Your windowsill may turn out to be the perfect nesting space for one of these birds.

The combination of nectar feeders and bright-colored flowers can attract hummingbirds as well. Window boxes filled with red flowers, hanging planters of fuchsia, petunias, or red ribbon streamers on your feeders can help alert hummingbirds to your balcony garden and the availability of food there.

Hanging baskets offer excellent advantages for balcony gardens. The baskets hang above the railing on your balcony, so they're clearly visible to birds. They move in the breeze, helping to draw attention to the garden and the feeders it contains. It's easy to change baskets with the seasons, removing a plant at the end of its blooming season and replacing it with a late season bloomer.

Your balcony has a weight limit, so choose plants that will not tax the structure of the platform. Take into consideration the weight of the soil, the pot, and the amount of water the tree will need. All together, this may approach one hundred pounds or more—the weight of a small person. Add several of these, and you may be approaching the balcony's limits. Instead of heavy trees, use flowering vines and a small trellis to create a wall effect. Remember to include your own weight in the calculation, and that of any guests who may join you on the balcony.

Black-eyed Susans naturalize easily in your garden.

3 Flowers and Ground Plants

Which flowers attract birds? The answer spans a wide range of blooms of many colors, shapes, and sizes, from the shaggy-top bee balm and bergamot that bring in the hummingbirds to the seed-laden centers of sunflower and coneflower.

Plant an assortment that includes tall-growing flowers with strong stalks, like black-eyed Susan, milkweed, blazing star and Joe-Pye weed, where sparrows and blackbirds can perch as they feed on the seeds embedded in the blossoms.

Bright red flowers with deep hearts, like cardinal flower, bee balm and columbine, attract hummingbirds that reach down into the cup to drink the nectar pooled inside. Orange flowers catch the eyes of orioles—especially jewelweed and the climbing trumpet vine, with its cupped flowers that provide the sweet centers that attract these flamboyantly marked birds. (We'll talk more about attracting orioles in Chapter 6.)

Milkweed, butterfly milkweed, lupine, and Joe-Pye weed all provide the added benefit of attracting butterflies, especially the monarchs that migrate through in spring and fall.

The best part about all of these native plants is that nearly all of them are perennials, so what you plant this spring will come back stronger every year. Ask your garden center or nursery for these and other native plants that grow well in your area.

Consult Appendix B: Northeast Hardiness Zone Map on page 208 to determine your hardiness zone.

FLOWERS

BEE BALM (*MONARDA DIDYMA*)

A summer bloomer, this red, pink, purple, or white flower attracts both hummingbirds and butterflies. The plants multiply readily, making this a welcome addition to a natural garden. The plants grow to heights of about 3 feet. Bee balm can thrive in wet soil or in drier conditions, depending on the variety you've chosen. The plants are

Bee balm

susceptible to mildew if they cluster too closely together, so break apart and separate the plants every other summer to expand your bed and give them breathing room.

Zones 4–8, full sun to partial shade, blooms in mid- to late summer

BLACK-EYED SUSAN (*RUDBECKIA GOLDSTURM*)

While plants in the *rudbeckia* family are usually short-lived perennials, black-eyed Susans re-seed themselves annually, so you may never notice a gap in the flowers' lifespan. Once they begin blooming, they keep producing golden-yellow blossoms right into the fall. Many flowers mean many seeds for hungry sparrows, chickadees, titmice, jays, and other seed-eaters, which will continue to visit the dead heads throughout the late fall and winter. You'll see plenty of these along the roadsides and in open meadows throughout the late summer as well.

Black-eyed Susan

Zones 4–8, full to partial sun, blooms midsummer to fall

BLANKETFLOWER (*GAILLARDIA ARISTATA*)

Bursting into bloom in late spring and sustaining flowers into the fall, these bright, showy blossoms stand up to hot summers. The plants thrive in sandy soil, and once they are in your garden, they will continue to fill in whatever area you allow them to enter—hence the name "blanket flower." You will find lots of varieties of this species, including some that are solid yellow, but they all have a prominent seed cone in the center that brings in the birds.

Zones 5–8, full sun, blooms late spring to fall

Blanketflower

BLAZING STAR (*LIATRIS SPICATA/ LIATRIS ASPERA*)

Dense blazing star (*spicata*) and rough blazing star (*aspera*) bloom from late summer to fall, their tall spires shooting up in mid-summer and taking their time to develop before bursting open. Both varieties are most at home in open spaces, native to prairies and meadows and found growing wild in tight bunches in moist wetland habitats. Goldfinches come to its purple flowers to nibble out the seeds, just as they do to the more common (invasive) thistle plants in many open fields. You may find this plant under the names prairie gay feather, Kansas gay feather, blazing star, or button snakewort.

Dwarf blazing star

Zones 3–8, full sun, blooms late summer to fall

BUTTERFLY MILKWEED (*ASCLEPIAS TUBEROSA*)

Gorgeous clusters of bright orange blossoms make this plant a favorite in gardens throughout the region. Plants usually bloom in their second year after planting, so if yours don't give you a great show in their first summer, give them a second chance a year later. They attract lots of bugs and beetles, which in turn attract insect-eating birds, so these plants can be a good tool for bringing in warblers

Butterfly milkweed

and other seasonal songbirds. Like other milkweed plants, this one produces pods filled with seeds that float away on the air after the pod bursts open in fall, so it may pop up in new places in your garden (or your neighbors' gardens) the following year.

Zones 3–8, full sun, blooms midsummer

CANADA GOLDENROD
(*SOLIDAGO CANADENSIS*)

A tall, nodding plant that forms a bright backdrop to a garden, this well-known resident of open fields grows as tall as four feet, and it will spread and form colonies if you have wide-open areas in your yard. It's fairly easy to control, however, if you spend a little time pulling out young plants at the beginning of the growing season to keep your goldenrod localized. Expect high clusters of small yellow flower heads along blooming branches. In addition to birds plundering the seeds, deer may come to browse your goldenrod in fall and winter.

Zones 3–8, full sun, blooms late summer to fall

Canada goldenrod

CARDINAL FLOWER (*LOBELIA CARDINALIS*)

Crimson, cupped blossoms on three-foot stalks attract hummingbirds like magic, and the fact that cardinal flower blooms after many other plants have faded makes it a particularly important part of a bird lover's garden. It can be a little tricky to keep this plant healthy in your garden, however, as it needs constantly moist soil. Plant it around your pond or near enough to a birdbath that it absorbs the regular overflow. Keep your pets away from this plant, as all parts of it are poisonous to mammals.

Zones 2–8, sun to partial shade, blooms late summer to early fall

Cardinal flower

CANADIAN (OR WILD) COLUMBINE (*AQUILEGIA CANADENSIS*)

Whether you choose the red columbine for your hummingbird garden or one of this versatile plant's many other shades, you'll find columbine to be a dependable plant that blooms every spring. Columbine of one kind or another grows in just about every region of North America. Look for it in shades of yellow, red, white, purple, blue-green, or pink. Positioned downward to attract hummingbirds, these plants also produce seeds that interest other birds.

Wild columbine

Zones 3–8, full sun to partial shade, blooms late spring to early summer

COMMON MILKWEED (*ASCLEPIAS SYRIACA*)

Quite a number of milkweed varieties are available from garden centers, so keep an eye out for swamp and rose milkweed as well as common. Any of these are appropriate for your native New England garden, and they all will attract butterflies, bees and birds when they bloom in midsummer. Milkweed is aggressively invasive, with pods that burst in early fall and send fluffy wings bearing seeds far and wide on the autumn air. Keep an eye out for milkweed sprouts in other parts of your garden and yard the following spring.

Common milkweed

To keep the plants at bay, snip off the seedpods while they are still green, before they burst open. (If you want to plant seeds next spring, let the pods dry on the plant, and then bring them in and break them open to collect the seeds. Store them in a dry place until next spring.)

Zones 4–8, full sun to partial shade, blooms in midsummer

COMMON YARROW (*ACHILLEA MILLEFOLIUM*)

Pink or white, yarrow produces clouds of flowers at the tops of three-foot stalks, and it will crowd out weeds by spreading furiously in your garden year after year. Birds come to yarrow for the seeds it produces, while bees and butterflies come for its pollen, making this a strong candidate for a nature lover's garden. If you transplant or pull clumps of this plant, be sure to wear gardening gloves, as it can produce an allergic skin reaction.

Zones 3–8, full sun, blooms late spring to early fall depending on the zone and weather

Common yarrow

CORAL BELLS (*HEUCHERA*)

A native plant that thrives in a rock garden, along a path, or in a sun-dappled woods, coral bells bloom in shades of red and pink, sometimes with purple foliage. Place these plants close together to get a bed of coral bells, allowing several hummingbirds to feed at a time. After the first bloom, cut the stalks back to promote a second blooming later in the season.

Zones 4–8, sun to partial shade, blooms June to August

Coral bells

JEWELWEED (*IMPATIENS CAPENSIS*)

Brilliant orange and yellow-gold blossoms bring in orioles, hummingbirds, and other colorful birds to consume

Jewelweed

the nectar and seeds of this easily propagating plant. Jewelweed needs constantly moist soil, so it's the perfect plant to ring your pond or mound under your birdbath if you have a continuous drip system (see Chapter 7). Where there's one jewelweed plant, there will soon be many more, so choose an area that allows it to spread—or deadhead the blossoms before they drop their seeds if you want to contain your jewelweed to one area.

Zones 4–8, partial to full shade, blooms midsummer to early fall

JOE-PYE WEED (*EUPATORIUM MACULATUM,* *EUTROCHIUM PURPUREUM*)

An excellent plant to place around a post for high feeders, this tall, bushy stalk produces wide masking foliage, growing up to four feet by late spring. It blooms in masses of clustered pink, magenta or purple flowers, which in turn produce seed heads that attract all kinds of small birds. Bees and butterflies love a good Joe-Pye weed as well, and will attend to the blooms for weeks on end. Despite its presence in wetlands and open fields, this plant needs an average amount of water.

Zones 5–8, full sun to partial shade, blooms late summer to early fall

Joe-Pye weed

AMERICAN MAYAPPLE (*PODOPHYLLUM PELTATUM*)

Also known as mandrake root, the plant featured in so many fairy tales involving witchcraft, mayapple carpets a woodland floor in spring and produces a waxy white flower with a spiny yellow center. Birds, butterflies and bees love this spring bloomer, and its leaves provide cozy cover for ground-feeding species like sparrows, finches, juncos, buntings, and robins. Plant seeds in fall or rhizomes right after the last frost to catch the mid-spring bloom.

Zones 3–8, partial to full shade, blooms in early to mid-spring

American mayapple

NEW ENGLAND ASTER (*SYMPHYOTRICHUM NOVEA-ANGLIA*)

Few sights are more welcome than the deep purple blooms and yellow centers of New England's namesake fall flower, and while the aster's blossoms are a harbinger of the fall harvest, they join with goldenrod to create stunning wine-and-gold landscapes. You'll attract migrating monarch butterflies and small birds with these clusters of small flowers, while deer turn up their noses at this plant. Plant seeds in fall or buy plants in midsummer to bring this riot of fall color to your yard.

Zones 3–8, full sun to light shade, blooms late summer to late fall

New England aster

PURPLE CONEFLOWER (*ECHINACEA PURPUREA*)

Officially a member of the daisy family, this drought-tolerant perennial grows wild in prairies and open wooded areas throughout much of eastern North America. Sparrows, titmice, chickadees, cardinals, jays, and other seed-eating birds love the protruding seed heads these flowers offer up, seeking them out almost as soon as the blossoms reach their full bloom. Put in at least a dozen plants to start your garden; add more each year to create a substantial bed.

Zones 4–8, full sun, blooms in midsummer

Purple Coneflower

TICKSEED OR PLAINS COREOPSIS
(*COREOPSIS TINCTORIA*)

Coreopsis varieties are found throughout North America, and many cultivars provide deep red or bright orange centers surrounded by yellow outer petals. The solid yellow variety is native to the northeastern states, but this and any of the cultivars will bring in birds to nibble at the dead seed heads as natural food grows scarce in winter. The nodding heads and easy propagation make this an excellent addition to a tall garden of native flowers.

Zones 2–8, full sun to partial shade, blooms in midsummer

Tickseed coreopsis

TRUMPET VINE (*CAMPSIS RADICANS*)

Also know as trumpet creeper or hummingbird vine, this climbing plant loves a good trellis or deck post around which it can wrap itself. Its leaves are among the last to appear in spring, and it will be late summer before you see its fluted, creamy orange flowers—but once they appear, the hummingbirds will become your most regular feathered visitors. Once it's established, this sure-fire plant will be with you for decades. Keep its new growth trimmed in summer to prevent it from taking over your yard.

Zones 4–8, sun to partial shade, blooms in late summer

Trumpet vine

WILD BERGAMOT (*MONARDA FISTULOSA*)

The lavender cousin to bee balm, bergamot brings another shade to your tall flower garden while attracting birds, bees and butterflies to its fluffy, fragrant blooms. You've seen this flower in open fields in late spring and summer,

Wild bergamot

and it's one of the good scents you smell in wild green spaces if you hike in July and August. Bergamot is a vigorous plant that will self-seed throughout your garden, so keep this in mind, if you plan to leave the seed heads on the plants over the winter to allow birds to feed.

Zones 3–8, full sun to partial shade, blooms early summer to early fall

GROUND COVERS

Ground covers present a host of opportunities to reduce the maintenance required in a garden or yard while providing shelter and hiding places for birds. They also provide an easy and thorough way to cover sizable areas of lawn with a permanent solution that doesn't need weekly mowing. Best of all, a native ground cover will block falling weed seeds, keeping them from germinating in your garden.

Choose a different ground cover for each area of your garden if you wish, or mix several as replacements for your lawn. Over time, the plants will take advantage of the gaps between your trees, shrubs, and perennials, establishing the ground cover as the foundation of your garden.

Even these self-sustaining carpets of green require some maintenance as they grow. Most ground covers are invasive, extending their territory beyond the space you may have allotted for them. Regular pruning and trimming will keep your lush greenery in check—but keep an eye out for one ground cover sending shoots out into another. If you don't want your covers to mix, add low stone walls between one plant and the next, and trim each species along the edge of the stone.

As you choose ground covers, check with your garden center or online to see if your choice is deciduous or coniferous. Some ground covers die back completely in winter, while others remain green year-round. Some also produce flowers, adding another dimension to your spring color.

LILY OF THE VALLEY (*CONVALLARIA MAJALIS*)

Just a foot tall, the dark green leaves of lily of the valley remain shiny and verdant throughout the summer months. In late spring, established plants produce tiny white cuplike blossoms that hang facing downward—a treat to view when a field of this plant carpets a hillside or serves as the floor of a backyard. Lily of the valley spreads

Lily of the valley

on its own, but it takes quite a number of plants to start a bed. Considering filling a small area of your garden with this and surrounding it with other ground covers or blooming plants.

Zones 4–8, light shade, blooms mid-spring

VIRGINIA CREEPER (*PARTHENOCISSUS QUINQUEFOLIA*)

This common plant is native to eastern North America and produces small, greenish flowers in late spring, and berries in late summer (that are great for robins and mockingbirds, but toxic to humans). The vines also produce a sap that can cause skin irritation in some people. Left to its own devices, this plant climbs trellises, poles, and trees. It makes a hardy ground cover on slopes and in wide-open areas. In fall, its leaves turn a brilliant red.

Virginia creeper

Zones 3–8, partial shade to full sun, blooms in spring

STONECROP (*SEDUM*)

Stonecrop, more popularly known as sedum, can be found in a wide variety of forms. Its slow-growing but hardy hold on your garden's soil makes it both attractive and useful as it wanders between rocks or edges around tree roots. Sedum protects your garden from erosion, especially on hillsides, growing low and close to the ground in compact clusters. Its flowers form tight bunches of seeds when the bloom

Stonecrop

is over, making them a good source of food for ground-feeding sparrows, juncos, thrushes, and doves.

Zones 4–8, partial shade to full sun, blooms in late summer

ALLEGHENY SPURGE
(*PACHYSANDRA PROCUMBENS*)

The native cousin to the exotic pachysandra so many people plant in their yards, Allegheny spurge grows more slowly than the Japanese version. Its leaves add fall color to northern landscapes, then drop off and grow again in early spring. In its lower territory in the southern states, the leaves remain green year-round. Separate the plants in spring or fall to spread the ground cover more quickly. While the plant does not provide food for birds, its broad

Allegheny spurge

leaves give cover to ground-feeding birds including sparrows, thrushes, and thrashers.

Zones 5–8, partial to full shade, no flowers

JUNIPER (*JUNIPERUS*)

Low growing, tolerant of bad soil, drought resistant, and not especially tasty to your neighborhood deer, this plant makes the perfect ground cover. The bluish green foliage remains throughout the year, turning a little bit purple in colder climates. For homes near the ocean, juniper is comfortable in sandy soil and remarkably resistant to salt spray. Juniper produces berries that are particularly attractive to waxwings, mockingbirds, and robins, as well as grosbeaks and bluebirds in winter.

Zones 4–8, full sun to light shade, no flowers

Juniper

Trees and shrubs offer shelter and food to birds.

4 Trees and Shrubs

As you choose the trees and shrubs that will become the anchoring features in your garden, remember some of the key elements birds need: food, shelter, as well as places to rest and nest. Trees and shrubs that provide fruit, nuts, or seed-filled cones quickly rise to the top of the list, while trees with dense foliage that masks nesting birds' location from predators are excellent choices for your backyard birds.

At the same time, think about your own needs as well. You want to be able to see the birds that arrive in your yard, so place trees and shrubs where you can view them from your window during winter months, and from your deck, porch, or patio in the warmer months. Equally important, you want your trees and shrubs to be positive additions to your yard, bringing beauty as well as bird activity.

The northeastern states enjoy a substantial list of long-lived, highly productive trees and shrubs, many of which produce fruit from late summer through the fall. Nut-bearing trees like oaks will bring in the birds, especially acorn-loving blue jays. Conifers—cone-producing trees—work year-round to attract birds, especially in winter. Your pines, spruces, and firs may bring in winter finches like crossbills and redpolls.

A word to the wise: Be careful to avoid berry-producing vines that are not native to your area. It's easy to mistake a native vine for one that actually will strangle other plants that belong in this area. For example, American bittersweet is native to the northeast; it's an endangered, self-regulating plant that produces yellow and orange berries in fall, creating a fine spectacle in your garden. Oriental bittersweet, however, looks very similar but is highly invasive, blocking out and killing other plants in its path. If you're not sure what you're buying, ask at your favorite nursery or garden center. (Many nurseries are committed to native plants, and will not stock or sell invasive species.)

Consult Appendix B: Northeast Hardiness Zone Map on page 208 to determine your hardiness zone.

AMERICAN CRANBERRY VIBURNUM (VIBURNUM TRILOBUM)

Big, splashy, 4-inch white flowers precede clusters of small, bright crimson berries that last well into the fall—because thrashers, mockingbirds, titmice, robins, sparrows, bluebirds and other fruit-eaters will wait until late winter to devour them, allowing the sun and cold to ferment the berries. By fall, the berries turn blue-black and the shrub's foliage turns from green to a maroon that borders on purple, making this a stunning addition to your yard's autumn spectacle. This viburnum grows to 8 to 10 feet, making it a candidate for a hedge or privacy border.

Zones 3–7, full sun to partial shade, blooms mid-spring

American cranberry viburnum

AMERICAN HOLLY *(ILEX OPACA)*

Glossy, dark green leaves that stay green all winter, and shiny, cherry-red berries—it's no wonder that this iconic plant has become a symbol of the winter holidays. This holly requires at least one male shrub for every small group of females. Without a male plant, the females will not produce berries. Both male and female plants bloom, covering themselves with small white flowers in spring. By midsummer, the berries appear on the female shrubs. Look for mockingbirds, catbirds,

American holly

thrashers, robins, and bluebirds eating the berries in winter.

Zones 5–8, full sun or partial shade, blooms in spring

CHOKECHERRY (*PRUNUS VIRGINIANA*)

Growing to just 20 feet tall, chokecherry can be found in the wild in hedgerows, on the edges of fields, and in open

Chokecherry

woods. The bright purple-red cherries—smaller than a conventional cherry—follow masses of white flowers that cover the tree in spring. You'll find that they're not sweet like the cherries we bake into pies. Instead, they have an astringent quality that makes humans pucker. Waxwings, titmice, bluebirds, robins and mockingbirds wait for the fruit to ferment before they arrive to enjoy it.

Zones 2–6, full sun to partial shade, blooms mid-spring

COMMON ELDERBERRY (*SAMBUCUS NIGRA L. SSP. CANADENSIS*)

Keep the soil moist under this shrub, and it will reward you with clouds of white blossoms and plenty of purple berries. You'll have birds all winter as long as the fruit lasts, with visits from robins, waxwings, chickadees, finches, mockingbirds, grosbeaks, titmice and woodpeckers. Be

Common elderberry

sure to choose the elderberry species named here, which produces purple or blue berries. The red berries of other species are toxic to humans. Other parts of this plant are edible: Dip a flower cluster in batter and fry it up for breakfast, or add the petals to batter for pancakes.

Zones 3–8, full sun, blooms in late spring/early summer

COMMON WILD ROSE (ROSA VIRGINIANA)

A pink rose with five petals and a yellow center, the truly wild rose is a native of the eastern United States—but the rose you may be able to acquire for your yard may not be strictly "wild." Many cultivated species have been developed based on the native, while roses you may see in the wild can be remnants of residences long gone. In fall, this rose produces bright orange-red hips that contain seeds. House, purple, and goldfinches flock to devour these over

Common wild rose

the winter. (Don't be confused by multiflora rose, a highly invasive shrub that has taken over coastline parks and forests throughout New England.)

Zones 5–8, full sun, blooms in June

EASTERN SERVICEBERRY (*AMELANCHIER CANADENSIS*)

One of the first trees to produce flowers in spring, this tree will grow to 20 to 25 feet. Its fuzzy grayish leaves led to its other common name, downy serviceberry. Its round, purple and red berries are edible for humans as well as birds; they may attract squirrels as well as cedar waxwings, robins, mockingbirds, cardinals and many others. In addition to its berries, this serviceberry turns yellow, gold, orange and red in fall, a welcome ornament in your yard before the winter snows.

Eastern serviceberry

Zones 4–7, full sun or partial shade, blooms in early spring

EASTERN WHITE PINE (*PINUS STROBUS*)

One of the most common conifers in New England (in fact, it's the state tree of Maine), eastern (or northern) white pine once covered the area as part of the vast forests that blanketed the northeastern states. You will be doing your area a favor by bringing white pines into your garden—these trees are quick to reach maturity, and often grow to heights beyond 200 feet. The long cones

Eastern white pine

that the white pine produces are a favorite food of red crossbills, and they also attract squirrels, chipmunks, and woodpeckers. Grackles, mourning doves, chickadees, nuthatches, and woodpeckers often choose white pine for their nesting sites. Nurseries sell cultivars that are bred to grow only to 30 to 50 feet tall, so you can have one even if your yard cannot host a very large tree.

Zones 3–8, full sun to partial shade

HAWTHORN (*CRATAEGUS*)

A member of the rose family (from which it gets its thorns), America's native hawthorns grow wild in wooded areas and protected lands across the country. Hawthorn blooms in early spring before its leaves appear, creating quite a spectacle with its cloud of white flowers. Its second act arrives in summer as big berries with red dots

Hawthorn (Dotted variety pictured here)

burst into production. Look for cedar waxwings, robins, bluebirds, and red-winged blackbirds eating these berries.

Zones 6–8, full sun to partial shade, blooms late spring

NANNYBERRY (*VIBURNUM LENTAGO*)

A shrub or small tree that will top out at about twelve to fifteen feet, nannyberry produces clusters of white flowers that give way to dark blue berries. While the bark can smell a little funky, the overall effect brightens your garden and provides lots of yummy food for cedar waxwings, thrushes, mockingbirds, catbirds, towhees and other fruit-eating birds.

Nannyberry

Zones 2–8, sun to partial shade, blooms in late spring/early summer

NORTHERN HIGHBUSH BLUEBERRY (*VACCINIUM CORYMBOSUM*)

From Nova Scotia to Alabama and from Maine to Wisconsin, people and birds love northern blueberry. You may be reluctant to share the abundant fruit with your resident waxwings, robins, mockingbirds and bluebirds, so plant several shrubs. You'll have plenty of berries for everyone, and the additional bushes will aid the pollination process, increasing the yield. Keep the soil moist, and you should have good luck with this hardy native shrub.

Northern highbush blueberry

Zones 3–8, full sun or partial shade, blooms in late spring/early summer

MOCK-ORANGE (*PHILADELPHUS*)

Mock-orange blooms look like those on a real orange or lemon tree, but the resemblance ends with the blossom. The

Mock-orange

"fruit" of this shrub is not a sweet round orange, but a seed-filled capsule, a food of interest to some resident flickers, sparrows, and woodpeckers in winter. Orange-blossom-scented blooms cover the shrub in late spring, making it a particularly attractive addition to a northeastern yard.

Zones 4–8, full sun to partial shade, blooms in late spring

OAK (QUERCUS)

If you have room for a tree that will spread its boughs wide, and you want woodpeckers and blue jays in your garden, plant an oak tree or two and watch the birds arrive to plunder the acorns. Eastern black and eastern white oak, northern red oak, pin, burr and scarlet oaks are all native to the northeastern states, and any of these will provide you with abundant shade under bowers that grow as high as 80 feet. In fall, this tree's leaves will turn a brilliant red or gold. An oak is

Oak (Red oak pictured here)

a lifelong commitment, so stand warned: Your oak trees will outlive you, your children, and your grandchildren. Some known trees are more than 400 years old.

Zones 3–8, full sun to partial shade

PAGODA DOGWOOD (*CORNUS ALTERNIFOLIA*)

This sun-loving dogwood makes a large shrub or a small tree, producing white flowers in late spring. Blue-black fruit follows the flowers in late summer, hanging on

long after the leaves have turned purple-red as the winter approaches. Virtually all fruit-eating birds love dogwood berries, so watch for grosbeaks, waxwings, bluebirds, jays, towhees and other fall migrants or overwintering species.

Zones 3–8, full sun to partial shade, blooms in late spring

Pagoda dogwood

RED OSIER DOGWOOD (*CORNUS STOLONIFERA*)

One of the most distinctive shrubs in the dogwood family, red osier's construction involves dozens of bright red canes rising from a central source. The canes produce clusters of tiny, fluffy white flowers in spring, which give way to snow-white berries. The

Red osier dogwood

red stems and white berries make red osier a pleasure to see in frigid winter months. Mockingbirds, waxwings, robins, and grosbeaks devour its berries in late winter, when fruits with higher sugar content have been depleted.

Zones 3–8, full sun to partial shade, blooms in late spring

RED SPRUCE (*PICEA RUBENS*)

Native to northern New England and now found in all of the region's states, this spruce grows anywhere from fifty to 130 feet tall and produces small and tightly packed cones. More resistant to spruce budworm and other spruce-eating insects than the related black and white spruce varieties, this tree remains hardy literally for centuries, growing to a diameter of as much as sixty feet. You'll find woodpeckers, jays, and chickadees making this tree

Red spruce

their home, and white-winged crossbills derive as much as fifty percent of their diet from this tree.

Zones 3-8, full sun to partial shade

SMOOTH SUMAC *(RHUS GLABRA)* AND STAGHORN SUMAC *(RHUS TYPHINA)*

Spreading easily from the initial plant to cover a fence or a wall, sumac produces greenish flowers in tall and upward-pointed clusters. When the flowers fade, the real show begins: The cluster turns scarlet with fruit, maturing to a rusty red as fall approaches. But wait, there's more: Now the leaves turn as red as the fruit, giving you a spectacular fall show. Chickadees, robins, and bluebirds will feast on this fruit all winter, while your long-lasting sumac seeds

Smooth sumac

may attract such wonders as ruffed grouse, ring-necked pheasant, gray catbird, wood and hermit thrushes, and eastern phoebe. Watch out for American crows and European starlings plundering your sumac as well.

Zones 4–8, full sun to partial shade, blooms in late spring

Hairy woodpecker on suet feeder

5 Your Bird Buffet

You've planted plenty of natural food in your bird lover's garden, but there's nothing like a bird feeder with the right kind of seeds, nuts, suet, fruit, or nectar to bring the birds out from behind the leaves to give you a really good look. Adding a few well-placed feeders to your yard will tempt the birds to perch or hover where you can see and enjoy them.

WHAT BIRDS EAT

While survival instincts extend some birds' diets during the months when their first-choice foods may be scarce, generally birds are specialists when it comes to seed, suet, nectar, and the delicacies we provide at our feeding station smorgasbord.

Many of the most colorful and tuneful birds will not approach feeders at all. Warblers, vireos, flycatchers, kingbirds, gnatcatchers, and a wide range of other birds are insectivores, beginning their migration south as soon as the bugs begin to wane at summer's end. These birds may come to your yard if you have a healthy population of yummy insects, but they are more likely to remain in the wild where their appetites are more easily satisfied.

A handful of bird species are generalists in their diet, feeding on hard-shelled seeds when these treats are available, but turning to berries and insects during nesting, feeding, and fledging their young. Cardinals and grosbeaks top this list, catching their food as they need it and frequenting feeders when their reproductive schedule allows it.

Sparrows and chickadees are voracious seed eaters. Pine siskins are often found at seed feeders, as are grackles and blackbirds. Cardinals and jays choose various kinds of seed before many other foods found in the wild. Finches of all colors prefer nyjer seed—also known as thistle seed, though it has no relationship to the actual thistle. This light, slender seed holds little interest for other birds or squirrels.

Some birds prefer to feed on the ground, but will come to a well-stocked platform feeder that simulates ground-feeding behavior. You may see juncos, jays, grackles, titmice, and blackbirds come to a platform feeder. Doves are fond of platforms as well, especially the ubiquitous mourning doves. If the feeder contains a mix of peanuts and sunflower seed, nuthatches and some woodpeckers may make occasional stops as well.

Hummingbirds, the most desirable of all feeder birds, love nectar, the basic sugar water mix with which we fill their feeders. Orioles are also nectar lovers, and are more likely to come to nectar feeders with perches that allow these larger birds to linger. Even more than nectar, orioles are very fond of fruit—especially oranges. Slice an orange in half and place it on an oriole feeder, or in the crook of a tree branch.

Woodpeckers and nuthatches go nuts for suet, whether it's the pure stuff you buy from your butcher or the packaged cakes that slip easily into suet cages. Jays, grosbeaks, house sparrows, and chickadees will come for suet blends that include seeds and nuts, while titmice and house finches may put in appearances to nibble as well. Starlings are also big fans of suet. Your winter woodpeckers may suddenly be crowded off your suet feeder by starlings as the first signs of spring arrive.

Birding Tip: Keep Feeding Year-round

Common wisdom suggests that we should stop feeding birds in summer or fall, when natural food sources are plentiful. The truth is that birds will supplement their diets at your feeders while taking advantage of the food around them. Go ahead and continue to feed year-round; the birds will take what they need and go elsewhere for the rest.

CHOOSING SEED BLENDS

Cheaper is not better! Those inexpensive seed blends contain lots of seed that birds throw out of your feeder and onto the ground. These add pounds to the seed bag, but do nothing to attract interesting birds to your yard (and they may attract mice and rats). Even the squirrels turn up their noses at fillers like golden millet, red millet, and flax.

Better blends that contain a variety of seeds include sunflower, safflower, and white proso millet and will attract birds' attention. White proso millet is popular with

Undesirable blend

Better blend

Pure sunflower seeds

Nyjer seed

many birds, including chickadees, doves, jays, finches, towhees, buntings, juncos, and some sparrows. Some premium blends contain bits of calcium carbonate, which female birds need for the formation of sturdy eggshells. The birds you attract will make you glad that you chose the pricier blend.

Sunflower seeds are the most favored seed by the widest variety of birds. Choose from the softer-shelled black oil sunflower seeds, or black striped sunflower seeds, which are harder for some birds to open. Filling your feeders with black striped sunflower seeds can be a quick deterrent to house sparrows and blackbirds, which prefer the softer seeds.

Nyjer seed (also known as thistle seed, although it does not come from thistle plants) generally comes from countries in Africa. It's been treated so that it will never sprout, making it a risk-free backyard offering. This seed is a little more expensive than most blends, but it's a magnet for American goldfinches, house and purple finches, pine siskins, and other small birds that thrive in areas of tall grasses. Nyjer seed requires a feeder with smaller holes than the feeders you fill with sunflower and other seeds.

You will see many varieties of seed mixes at your local do-it-yourself, hardware, farm supply, and birding specialty stores, with names for their mixes that are meant to tempt your wallet. Be wary of fancy naming strategies; instead, read the bags and see exactly what's in the mix before buying. Watch out for seed blends that include chemicals advertised as "vitamin supplements." Generally, these are meant for caged birds that cannot hunt for their own food. Wild birds get their nutrition from the foods they eat, so these chemicals are unnecessary.

SUET

Extraordinarily popular with a wide variety of bird species, including woodpeckers, sapsuckers, nuthatches, and even warblers, suet has become the favorite offering of backyard birders. With its rise in desirability has come a startling selection of varieties, all pressed into cakes, rendered for year-round use, and readily available in discount stores and supermarkets as well as birding specialty stores.

Suet provides birds with a concentrated source of protein, one of the most important elements in helping them maintain energy throughout the nesting and breeding season. Overwintering birds require energy for warmth—in fact, some birds must eat constantly all day

Red-bellied woodpecker feeding from a log feeder with holes stuffed with suet

to take in the protein and fat they need to survive a frigid winter's night. They replenish their stores of fat by frequenting your suet feeders, making winter bird gardens a treat for nuthatch and woodpecker lovers. The same birds will return during the spring and summer, bringing mouthfuls of suet to their nestlings. Suet blends that contain fruit and nuts provide important nutrients to baby birds.

You can buy cakes of pure suet, or suet blended with seed, nuts, fruit, or even insects. Blends with fruit and insects can attract wrens and spring warblers, especially if migrating birds arrive before insects become plentiful. Orioles may take an interest in berries or orange essence mixed into the suet. Blends with nuts attract chickadees, nuthatches, grosbeaks, sparrows, and jays. Just about any kind of suet cake will bring woodpeckers to your yard, while house sparrows, starlings, and grackles will establish residency to feast at your suet feeder.

Suet cakes from reputable manufacturers are processed to remove impurities that make raw suet melt or spoil. These rendered cakes are stable up to about 100 degrees Fahrenheit, making them appropriate for all climates except for the hottest desert areas. Some manufacturers refine suet even further to make it usable in temperatures above 100 degrees. Look for varieties with "No Melt" on the label.

Pre-packaged suet cakes

In winter, you may prefer to use suet purchased from your local butcher, supplying birds with animal fat in its purest form. The greatest advantage to this is that squirrels are generally disinterested in the stuff, while they will hang upside down for long intervals to chow down on manufactured suet and seed cakes. As the weather gets warmer, however, switch back to commercially made suet cakes, or you will have a smelly, rancid mess in your suet feeders.

NECTAR

Everyone wants tiny, bee-like hummingbirds in their yard, and the promise of nectar-seeking orioles can have backyard birders getting up at dawn just to watch their nectar feeders.

It's easier than you might think to make your own nectar—and infinitely preferable to the powdered or bottled varieties you find in stores. It takes about ten minutes, and homemade nectar provides the nutritional balance birds need to keep their energy up throughout the nesting, breeding, and migration seasons. Commercial nectars contain additional ingredients beyond sugar, none of which improve the taste or benefits of the nectar itself.

A female ruby-throated hummingbird approaches a nectar feeder.

As your local weather warms and the sun heats your nectar feeders, you will need to change the nectar every couple of days to keep it fresh. Sugar water ferments in heat—this is the basic principle involved in making beer and wine—and the soured brew is bad for the birds. To keep up with the demand, you can make gallons of nectar

Don't Add Red Food Coloring!

Most nectar feeders have red trim, so the birds will find them without enhancements. Researchers have found that hummers that eat food-color-enhanced nectar develop health issues and have shorter life spans. Don't add honey to your feeders, either— honey and water create exactly the environment bacteria need to thrive.

How to Make Nectar

Determine how much nectar your hummingbird feeder will hold.

- Add that much water to a saucepan.
- Stir in 1 part sugar to every 4 parts water—so if the feeder holds 2 cups of water, add ½ cup sugar.
- Bring the water to a boil. Stir until the sugar dissolves, and continue to boil for ten minutes.
- Let the water cool, and fill your feeder.

to have on hand, especially if you feed hummingbirds at many feeders and your tiny friends frequently empty your reservoirs. The nectar will keep in your refrigerator for several days, or longer in many cases.

Nectar feeders come in many shapes and sizes, but the birds don't care about the décor—as long as there's something red on the feeder to catch their eyes as they seek nourishment. If your feeder does not have red elements, tie a red ribbon around the top or hang red streamers from the bottom. The birds will spot it easily.

Oriole nectar feeders are often very similar to those that attract hummingbirds, except they may be larger and usually have orange trim. Orioles prefer to perch rather than hover, so feeders that provide a foothold will attract these stunning birds. You may find orioles coming to your hummingbird feeder to drink the nectar you offer—it's not critical that you have a separate nectar feeder. Orioles also feed on insects, fruit, jelly, and nectar produced by flowers.

FRUIT AND NUTS

From the first strawberries of early summer to the nuts that drop from trees in the fall, your backyard can supply birds with a steady, nutritious diet. By sharing the bounty of your shrubs and trees with the birds, you provide them with the kinds of foods for which they would forage on their own—and you get to watch them in action.

White-breasted nuthatch at peanut feeder

Many birds that devour insects from spring through fall find themselves without this basic sustenance in winter. Not all of these birds migrate to the balmy climate of Central and South America, however—in fact, some of these birds move southward from northern Canada to the northern United States, where they find alternative food sources among the nuts and berries that linger in the trees throughout the winter.

Others do not migrate at all, shifting their dietary focus from bugs and grubs to fruit, pinecones, and acorns to generate the energy they need to survive the winter. The American robin is just one of many species that will switch from invertebrates to berries, pinecones, or nuts over the winter. Northerners associate robins with the onset of spring, so they are often startled by the sudden appearance of dozens or even hundreds of robins in the middle of January. These birds have not started the migration early; they've probably been in the area all winter, feeding on juniper berries, the remaining serviceberries or holly, and the orange berries of the mountain ash.

In spring and summer, some birds—orioles and jays in particular—are readily attracted to fruits and jellies set out for them in your backyard. Baltimore and orchard orioles are quick to come to feeders filled with grape jelly.

Nuthatches and woodpeckers love to pick peanuts out of feeders. As the peanuts are fairly challenging to remove, the birds linger at these feeders for several minutes at a time, giving you plenty of opportunity to enjoy their long-billed exploration. Trees in your yard that produce black walnuts, acorns, or pinecones will attract a fascinating variety of jays and grosbeaks in fall and crossbills in winter, which dig seeds out from between pinecone scales with their uniquely shaped bills.

MEALWORMS

Most bird gardeners would not think to provide insects at their feeders—but when birds are busy raising their young in late spring and early summer, an easily accessible supply of dried bugs may ease the strain on busy mother birds. You can do a great service to your resident bluebirds, robins, wrens, and others by adding a dedicated platform feeder stocked with dried or live mealworms. These creatures provide nutrients including protein and vitamins A and B, which are important to a bird's health and longevity.

Mealworms are the larvae of the darkling beetle, cultivated by commercial growers and packaged for home bird feeding. It's easy to pour a supply of these into a platform feeder without handling the worms at all. You can purchase them at birding specialty stores, grain and

A female eastern bluebird grabs a mealworm from a feeder.

feed stores like CountryMax or Fleet Farm, and at some D-I-Y hardware chains. Fishing specialty stores also carry live and dried mealworms. Some suppliers also sell wax-worms, the larvae of bee moths, or fly larvae, which are smaller than either mealworms or waxworms. Any of these will attract insect-eating birds.

Live mealworms are the most effective in attract-ing birds, as their movement catches the eye quickly. To keep live mealworms in place, use a feeder with a slippery bottom and sides—a glass or hard plastic dish with sides at least 3 inches high. The mealworms will not be able to negotiate the slick sides, but they will keep attempt-ing to do so—and birds will see them moving and come in to eat. If the idea of storing live larvae in your refrig-erator is not particularly appealing, the roasted or dried mealworms still will attract birds, although it may take more time for the birds to find them.

Dried mealworms often come in plastic containers or bags and also come mixed with additional fruit flavors, or even with dried fruits like cranberries or raisins. As dried mealworms do not move, mixing them with fruits will help attract birds more quickly. Mix dried mealworms with a little vegetable or olive oil to make them look juicy and shiny. Place the feeder near a birdbath, recirculating pond, or fountain with moving water, to help the birds find it.

A tube feeder hangs from a shepherd's crook in a garden.

6 Bird Feeders

Birds are very adept at finding their own food in the wild, but like any other creature, they will take the path of least resistance to a good meal—especially if that meal is offered consistently and in quantity. The key to attracting a wide variety of bird species is to offer several different kinds of food, using different kinds of feeders in various locations throughout your backyard.

SEED FEEDERS

The most popular feeders with birds and bird lovers alike, seed feeders provide twofold benefits: They're easy to use, and they attract plenty of active and colorful birds to your yard.

Place your seed feeders where birds can benefit from the three things they need most: food, water, and shelter. A feeder on a post in the middle of a wide-open, mowed yard will attract fewer birds than a feeder positioned near the cover of shrubs or trees. Birds are constantly on the watch for predators like hawks and cats, so they will choose feeders that offer them instant hiding places behind leaves or among thorns.

Feeders should be spaced so that birds have room to maneuver between them. Some feeders provide many openings through which birds can access the seed; these may attract small flocks of finches or chickadees. Place the feeders at least 10 feet apart, to make sure there's plenty of room for all of the birds to rest and eat.

It's fine to place feeders close to windows, or even to hang them from your eaves on hooks or plant hangers. Just be sure to position the feeders over or near bushes that provide sheltering leaves and branches. You can also purchase a feeder hanger (also called a shepherd's crook) from a D-I-Y or birding specialty store, and hang your feeders in the middle of a bed of native flowers. The birds will be attracted first by the color of the blooms and potential for natural seeds. They will stay to feed on the seeds or nuts you provide, and will keep coming back as your flowers produce their own seeds.

Finally, take careful note of what's under your feeder. Keep in mind that active feeders produce a litter of shells, and that inevitably, birds will leave their droppings as well. If you're planning to hang a feeder on a porch or deck or very close to your house, be sure that the leavings will not mar any surface that you'd prefer to keep clean.

Larger birds like woodpeckers, doves, and jays cannot perch comfortably on a tube feeder, as their size and weight make it difficult for them to get to the seed once they've settled on a perch. Hopper feeders offer larger perches, more space between the bird and the seed dispensing hole, and a stable perch that does not sway so easily under their weight.

Choose feeders that you can take apart easily for cleaning. Some feeders allow ridges of seed to harden below the holes, making it necessary to get inside the feeder and clean out compacted seed regularly before it begins to decay. The more readily the feeder comes apart, the easier it will be for you to protect birds from molds that can cause illness.

PLATFORM FEEDERS

A wide variety of birds, both small and mid-sized, prefer to feed with both feet on the ground instead of perching or clinging to a feeder. Platform feeders provide a ground-like experience for juncos, doves, pigeons, migrating sparrows, and jays. These flat feeders allow birds to land on a stable structure and search for food on the surface, a more comfortable method than reaching into awkward holes on a tube feeder to pull out seeds.

A common grackle comes to a platform feeder mounted on a post.

Birds that feed on the ground will come to a seed-laden platform even if it's several feet off the ground. With this in mind, position your platform feeder where it's easy for you to see. This will give you great views of birds you may be missing when you watch from inside your home. Install the platform on top of a post or pole, but close enough to trees or bushes to provide quick cover when hawks circle over your yard.

The best platform feeders hold seed, nuts, and even mealworms between two layers of mesh or screen. The first layer keeps the seed from blowing away or being brushed off the feeder by messy eaters. The lower screen has a finer mesh, which allows rain to fall through to the ground while keeping the seed in place and relatively dry.

Placing a platform or tray feeder on the ground can help you attract birds to a specific place in your yard, where you can observe them easily from a window. Choose a feeder with legs that lift the tray a few inches off the ground, to allow rainwater to drain away from the seed. Migrating birds looking for food sources will see the commotion on the ground at your tray feeder, increasing the number of species in your yard during spring and fall.

In all cases, limit the amount of seed and nuts you place in a platform or tray feeder. Too much seed can clog the drainage holes or mesh, turning the food into a soggy mess that will not appeal to any bird.

NECTAR FEEDERS

Hummingbirds and orioles will come willingly to feeders that offer nectar. See Chapter 5 for an easy, no-food-coloring nectar recipe.

A nectar feeder hangs among tube-shaped flowers to help attract hummingbirds.

One of the best things about hummingbirds is that they don't mind being close to human beings. This means that you can place your nectar feeders right under the eaves of your house, or on your porch, deck, or patio, and enjoy hummingbirds up close throughout the spring and summer months. If you want to see your hummingbirds' reflective feathers light up like neon, put your feeders where they will catch the sun.

Hummingbirds will find your feeders quickly if they hang over or near tubular flowers like trumpet vine, cardinal flower, or bee balm. The hummingbirds will feed on the flowers and spot the red decorations on your feeder. As hummers spend their lives seeking new food sources, they will visit your feeder as part of their regular rounds.

Orioles are a little more skeptical of human presence, but the lure of sugar water is strong—so they will perch on nectar feeders even when they hang close to household windows and doors.

Bees and ants come when the nectar spills or leaks from the feeder. Once the sticky residue is on the outside of the feeder, there's no getting rid of the bugs except to take down the feeder, clean it, and move it about 30 feet away from its original spot. In addition, bees are attracted to the color yellow. Choose a nectar feeder that does not feature yellow bee guards.

SUET FEEDERS

Many birds love suet, but you're probably feeding with this natural fat product because you want woodpeckers, nuthatches, creepers, and other tree-clinging birds to come to your yard. If you hang a suet feeder in the middle of your mowed yard or from a plant hanger off of your house's eaves, the birds you want are very unlikely to put in an appearance. Woodpeckers and nuthatches dig for insects within the bark of trees, so they may never notice a feeder in a clearing.

Birds that frequent suet feeders are accustomed to clinging vertically to tree bark, or even hanging upside-down as they scavenge along a tree branch for insects. They prefer the cage-style suet feeders that offer them wide, solid bars for clinging, with plenty of room between the mesh for their large bills to probe the suet.

For the best results, hang your suet feeders in trees close to the trunk, or tie the feeder to the trunk directly. Mounting a feeder in a tree or right on a tree trunk will

A downy woodpecker feeds on real suet in a cage feeder.

attract more woodpeckers and nuthatches more quickly. To fasten a suet cage to a trunk, don't drive nails into your tree—instead, secure the feeder using strong plastic-coated wire. Thread the wire through the back of the cage at the top and bottom, and twist the ends together on the other side of the tree. Once the feeder is secured, bring the suet out to the feeder to fill it. Remove the feeder and clean it at least once each season.

Feeders shaped like small logs are uniquely attractive to woodpeckers and other tree-clinging birds. Manufacturers make sticks of suet blended with nuts and seeds to insert into the holes of these feeders. You can use any kind of suet in these, however, as long as it's stuffed securely into the hole. (Suet on the ground attracts squirrels, not birds.) Hang one or more of these feeders in your trees to attract repeat visitors.

DIY: KEEPING FEEDERS CLEAN

Step 1: Remove Waste

Start by removing all the wet, sticky, or moldy seed from the bottom of the feeder. Use a stiff brush or long stick to reach into the bottom of the feeder. Tapping the bottom or sides will help loosen the residue. Deposit the waste into a trash basket lined with a plastic bag.

Step 2: Total Immersion

Fill your washtub or utility sink with enough hot water to immerse the feeder completely. Add one part bleach for every ten parts water. If you use two gallons of water (256 ounces), add about 26 ounces

of bleach. Disassemble your feeder as much as possible. Some feeders have removable perches or unscrew at the bottom; others may only have a removable top. Immerse the feeder and all of its parts completely in the hot water with bleach.

Step 3: Wash Thoroughly

Use a clean brush with a long handle to scrub the inside of the feeder. Make sure all of the seed residue, dust, and clinging mold gets cleaned out completely. Wash around

each of the seed dispensing holes, where birds perch and eat. Use a sponge or brush to clean any droppings off of the outside of the feeder.

Step 4: Dry Completely

Allow the feeder and all of its parts to dry thoroughly before reassembling and refilling. Filling a wet feeder with seed will only restart the spoilage process—as the seeds

come into contact with the moisture. If you need to get your feeders out quickly, use a blow dryer to hasten the drying process.

If you want to be sure that only tree-clinging birds feed on your suet, choose feeders that only offer access to the suet from the bottom. The only birds that can enjoy these feeders are those that can hang upside-down.

FEEDER MAINTENANCE

One of the most positive and effective things you can do for birds in your yard is also one of the simplest and least costly: clean your feeders regularly.

Seed feeders should be disinfected at least once a season, or any time that seed has had the chance to decay or become moldy inside the feeder. If birds eat the spoiled food, they can get sick.

Beyond the seed itself, birds often leave droppings on top of feeders and on perches. Studies have shown that bird droppings—especially house sparrow, pigeon, and starling droppings—may cause as many as 60 diseases in humans.

Nectar and jelly feeders should be washed thoroughly every time you refill them. As nectar hangs in a clear glass or plastic feeder in the sun, it begins the process of fermentation—essentially the same process through which breweries make beer. Hummingbirds don't care for fermented nectar, and they will avoid your feeder once they've tasted the sour stuff. Washing the feeder thoroughly will remove any residue, keeping your nectar fresh. It may take a while for the birds to trust your feeder again, but keep it full of fresh nectar regardless of whether you see hummingbirds.

Jelly and fruit feeders inevitably attract bugs, so washing these will remove any dead insects (usually ants).

If you're feeding with orange halves, cleaning the feeder will remove any mold the fruit may have fostered.

Keep your feeder cleaning tools separate from other tools in your basement, shed or garage. Create a kit that includes a long-handled feeder cleaning brush, sponge or other scrubber, measuring cup for bleach, and a long pointed stick to reach into the bottom of a tube feeder.

Pine siskins drink from a garden birdbath.

7 Neighborhood Watering Hole

There's no better way to attract birds to your yard than with moving water. Sources of water can be scarce for birds in areas with large human populations, especially in suburban areas or cities. Birds need water just as much as we do, so a clean water feature can bring mixed flocks to your yard on a regular basis.

In addition to hydration, birds need to clean themselves, and they will use your birdbath to do so. You'll see birds stand in shallow water, fluff their feathers to allow the water to reach their skin, and splash themselves with their wings. Some birds actually jump into the water and out again very quickly, seeming to bounce back and forth compulsively as they wet themselves thoroughly. Your water feature does a great service to the birds, and it's sure to provide you with some entertaining observations of bird behavior.

How do birds find the water? Moving water—a simple drip into an otherwise still pool, or a babbling recirculating fountain—will catch birds' eyes as they fly over your property.

Water has the added benefit of attracting birds that will not visit your feeders. Warblers and vireos will drop from their high perches in the treetops to visit your bird-bath, as will flycatchers, kingbirds, and all manner of sparrows.

CHOOSING A BIRDBATH

When you think of a birdbath, a single image may come to mind: the carved stone basin on a Grecian-looking pedestal, filled with standing water.

If this vision doesn't appeal to you, you're not alone. An entire industry has developed to provide us with a wide range of options that not only bring much-needed moisture to our birds, but also complement the style and layout of our gardens.

The carved stone birdbath is still available, but in new materials that stand up to the elements and in colors and models that add panache to your yard. If you've dreamed of having a small pond, it's easier than ever to create one, even in a yard with no natural water features. The sound of gently trickling water can be part of your backyard experience for a small investment and a minimum of technical effort.

PEDESTAL BIRDBATHS

Pedestals now come in a range of styles that can match any home, whether your house is a painted Victorian lady, a 1960s colonial, a turn-of-the-century Craftsman, or a new, ultra-modern home.

The majority of pedestal birdbaths are made from plastic or resin, which makes them virtually impervious to heat, cold, snow, and rain. For sheer durability, these are baths you can use as a centerpiece or accent for a garden of any size, whether you're tucking a birdbath into a corner of a small city yard or creating an expansive habitat filled with native flowers and shrubs.

A birdbath of cast stone or ceramic construction may be more to your taste. These offer no additional advantage to the birds, but they may match your home's style or be the perfect natural accent to

Pedestal birdbath made of modern materials

your garden. The potential for chipping, cracking, and storm wear are higher with natural materials.

While most manufacturers have taken water level into consideration in the design of their birdbaths, be sure to look closely at the depth of the bowl. The water should be shallow around the edges, so that birds can perch on the edge of the bowl and drink comfortably.

At the same time, the center of the bowl should be just deep enough to allow a sparrow to stand and bathe, fluffing out his feathers to splash water through to his skin. If the bowl is too deep, the birds will reject it as a water source.

If you've already got a pedestal birdbath and the water is too deep for comfort, place a rock in the center of the bowl. The rock should be large enough to rise above the water, giving birds a place to perch and drink, or to retain their footing while they splash themselves.

The two-tiered effect of the fountain and main bowl address the issue of water depth, giving birds more than one place to drink or bathe. The best of these are solar-powered, requiring no electrical lines or batteries. As the water circulates automatically, you can fill the reservoir once and refill when birds and evaporation lower the water level.

Resist the temptation to place the birdbath alone in the middle of your well-mowed yard. Like feeders and birdhouses, birdbaths need to be near trees or shrubs to allow the birds to escape to shelter. Leaves and other detritus may drop into the water, but the birds will actually stop to drink here, so the occasional clean-out of fallen twigs and bits will be well worth your effort.

DISH BIRDBATHS

Shaped like lily pads or painted with elaborate designs, dish birdbaths can sit on the ground, hang from planter hooks or shepherd's crook, fasten to the side of a deck railing, or stand at the edge of a patio.

Birds will go wherever they have a safe path of escape, so place your dish birdbath close to cover:

- Group potted plants around a birdbath on the ground or in a corner of your patio.
- Hang the birdbath next to a shrub or tree at the edge of your deck.
- Place it on the ground beneath a rosebush or hawthorn, where the thorns will protect the birds.
- Hang it in a pine tree with sheltering needles.

For the most part, dish birdbaths are less expensive than their pedestal or circulating counterparts. Equally important, dish birdbaths are easy to clean on a regular basis. Most can simply be lifted from a frame or hanger and emptied, or even brought into the house to wash in the basement laundry sink.

Generally, dish birdbaths are shallower than many pedestal baths, topping out at the ideal bird bathing depth of 1½ inches. If you've got your heart set on a dish that's deeper, remember the trick of placing a rock in the center to give birds an extra place to perch. Partially filling the birdbath also works well; check the water at least daily in hot weather and refill it if the sun evaporates the shallow pool.

A female house finch bathes in a plastic bowl birdbath.

Finally, look for dish birdbaths with ridges around the edges that provide footholds for the smallest birds.

YOUR OWN POND

Even very small spaces can accommodate a man-made pond, and the addition of this water feature to your yard can bring you many hours of pleasure—and many birds with which to share your small oasis.

A pond is more than a hole in the ground filled with water. It's a self-contained mini-ecosystem that you create to attract species that thrive in an aquatic habitat. Ponds do not need to be large, but they do need a well-constructed sand base and a strong rubber liner to keep the pond filled and contained.

Pond with man-made recirculating falling water feature

To keep your pond healthy and useful to birds, amphibians, and small animals, plan to include a pump that will keep the water moving. Without the pump, you risk creating a stagnant pool filled with algae and bacteria, instead of a lovely addition to your landscape. Worse, mosquitoes love standing water. A pump will circulate the water and could even create a small waterfall, generating the visual effect and soundscape you desire. The best pumps are noiseless, so no motor will mar the sound of trickling water.

You may choose simply to keep your water slightly agitated with a small pump, which is an effective safeguard against major buildup of surface scum and noxious organisms. If you dream of having your own waterfall, several manufacturers offer kits that make it fairly easy to create the cascading effect. How big a pump do you need for your pond? Experts say that your pump should be able to move half of your pond's capacity in an hour—so if your pond holds 200 gallons of water, you need a pump that flows at the rate of 100 gallons per hour.

Fountains actually lift the water above the pond's surface, so there are more elements to consider. Pond filters, pipes, and fittings all create resistance as the water moves through the fountain system. You will need a pump that can overcome this resistance. Your garden store can help you calculate the pressure you need. Be sure to ask lots of questions before you begin the installation, so you can eliminate costly issues up front.

Pond with fountain effect

CLEANING YOUR BIRDBATH

- Pour out all the water in the birdbath.

- Wear rubber gloves.

- Using a stiff bristle brush, scrub out all the soils and sludge accumulated in the bottom of the bath. Rinse with a garden hose.

- Wet down any bird droppings to make them soft, and scrub them off with the brush.

- Empty the droppings into a plastic garbage bag and discard.

- Finally, fill the birdbath with a solution of ¾ cup of household bleach to 1 gallon of warm water. Let it sit for ten to fifteen minutes to kill algae and bacteria. Rinse thoroughly.

Your pond will become a focal point around which you can create a delightful garden, so choose its location carefully. Avoid placing your pond directly under a tree. Flower petals, leaves, seeds, and fruit dropping from the tree will cover your pond regularly, giving you an unnecessary cleaning chore to do. If your pond is in a sunny spot, be sure to check the water level on hot days when evaporation could reduce the contents. Use your garden hose to add water.

Surround your pond with a rock border to cover the edge of the plastic liner, and also to define the edge and give small creatures a place to perch while they drink.

Think carefully about the plants that surround your pond—you'll need plants that grow best in very moist soil, or even right in the water. Create a stepped effect with low, mid-sized, and taller plants, giving your pond a natural appearance while providing suitable cover for birds of all kinds, whether they prefer to feed on the ground or to perch at the top of ornamental grasses or cattails. Cardinal flower, milkweed, jewelweed, and Joe-Pye weed are all good choices to place near a pond.

This tufted titmouse chose a fence-mounted box for its nest.

Audubon

8 Houses and Nesting

One of the most popular ways to bring birds into your yard is to invite them to nest. Providing birdhouses—typically called "nest boxes"—can encourage many bird species to make your yard a seasonal haven.

BIRDHOUSES

It's a common misconception that birdhouses become a bird family's home to which the birds will return year after year. With a few exceptions, this is rarely the case; birds use a nest box for laying eggs and raising young, usually vacating the premises once the young birds have left the nest. If a mated pair raises a second or third brood in a season, they usually move on to a new nesting location.

A shopping excursion for a birdhouse will reveal dozens of different varieties, from the very ornate to the simplest pine box with a hole in it. Choose whatever style of house you like to complement your yard and garden, but rest assured that birds are attracted to the size and position of the hole, not to the pretty paint or the detailed gingerbread trim on some very attractive nest boxes.

Why are there so many shapes and sizes? Different boxes attract different bird species. The choices are nearly as varied as the eighty bird species that will use nest boxes.

WHICH BIRDS USE BOXES

The birds' process of laying eggs, sitting on them until they hatch, and caring for their nestlings is so fascinating to us that we go to great lengths to invite the birds to do all of this in our own backyards.

Not every bird requires the assistance of a man-made nest box, however. In fact, the vast majority of birds do quite well in building their own nesting place and raising their young without any human intervention at all.

To make your yard as interesting as possible to the widest variety of nesting birds, choose nest boxes that are appropriate for birds that already nest and breed in your neighborhood.

Nest boxes are most attractive to cavity nesters: birds that look for holes that lead to snug, sheltered spaces in natural or manufactured places. A great many garden birds are cavity nesters, including house sparrows, wrens, nuthatches, woodpeckers, chickadees, titmice, tree swallows, some flycatchers, bluebirds, and purple martins. Cavity-nesting birds use the nest box for the sole purpose of raising young. Some birds may return to a nest box in winter to roost overnight or wait out storms in relative comfort.

Chickadees, nuthatches, and titmice all prefer cavities at about 5 to 6 feet off the ground. Choose a wooden box with a small hole, no larger than 1⅛ inches across, to allow these small birds to enter the nest box while keeping larger birds out. The nest should be in a tree, either tied to the trunk or suspended from a solid tree branch.

Bluebirds of all varieties prefer nest boxes on posts or poles in open land, where they have a wide view of the meadows or grasslands that surround them. If you live in a thickly developed suburban or city neighborhood, bluebirds are highly unlikely to find your nest box.

If your country yard does attract bluebirds, watch your nest box carefully for marauding house sparrows. These aggressive birds are known to drag young bluebirds out of the box and co-opt it for themselves. House sparrows are not protected by wildlife laws, so you are welcome—even encouraged—to pull a house sparrow nest out of your bluebird box and discard it.

Some birds prefer the open architecture of a shelf, roof beam, or even a retail store sign as the ideal nesting location. Robins are shelf nesters, choosing to nest at the tops of bushes, on open tree limbs, or on nesting platforms you can make or buy. Barn swallows and phoebes are also fond of this nesting style, often nesting exactly where you wish they would not.

When you know what birds you're likely to attract, visit your birding specialty store to get the best information on what boxes will interest your birds.

NEST BOXES THAT WORK

What makes a good nest box? While each bird species has its own preference for hole size and placement, some basic rules of thumb apply across most species.

Birds are attracted to what they know, so the best material for birdhouse construction is natural, untreated wood. Your nest box does not need a coat of paint or a chemical finish—in fact, the most practical nest boxes have no outer coating at all. Look for nest boxes made from coniferous (evergreen) wood like fir, pine, or cedar. If you're building your own box, there's no need to spend the extra money on pricey hardwoods—the birds are happy with the bargain-basement materials.

You can skip the sanding as well: Birds prefer an unfinished interior with rough walls. A slanted, overhanging roof helps deflect rain from the hole, and shades the interior from the sun.

Hole size is the most effective way to control the birds that have the chance to nest in your box. To keep house sparrows out of your nest boxes, make the hole no larger than 1⅛ inches. House wrens, chickadees, titmice, and nuthatches will still be able to enter. Bluebirds require a larger hole, up to 1½ inches, which is why they are so vulnerable to house sparrow home invasions. Songbirds like Carolina wrens can also use a hole this size.

Beyond the entrance hole, the nest box needs additional small ventilation holes to allow fresh air to enter once the nestlings have hatched. Small holes in the floor will allow moisture to escape when heavy rains hit, as they often do in humid climates during the summer months.

Don't add any perches outside the entrance hole—these are just an invitation to predator birds and invasive species like house sparrows to gain access. It's your job to keep predators from reaching into the box to steal eggs or grab nestlings. You have several choices for this. Buy or make a wooden hole extender that turns your birdhouse opening into a longer tube, making it too far for raccoons to reach. A cage-style hole extender also narrows the approach to the nest box opening, discouraging long-armed mammals, grackles and jays. These methods will deter house sparrows as well.

Finally, choose or make a box with a hinged roof and walls to allow you to open the box once the birds have moved out, and clean out the abandoned nest. The birds will not return to the nest, and the remains can attract parasites and other vermin that are not good for the birds.

When you choose a strong, durable nest box, you have the opportunity to see birds select this box, build a nest inside, incubate a clutch of eggs, and raise the young—all right in your own backyard.

SPECIES-SPECIFIC BOX REQUIREMENTS

We've talked about construction materials and the size of the opening, but these are just the initial steps in attracting birds to your nest box. Some of the eighty species that will use a nest box require very specific features before they'll turn your birdhouse into the seasonal family manse.

If you know exactly which species you'd like to have nesting in your box, you can create the perfect nesting environment for that bird. For example, purple martins are well known for their preference for social nesting. These birds need wide-open spaces like farmland or the "forever wild" of a wildlife refuge, where they can swoop and dart to catch insects—and a lake or pond with plenty of mosquitoes will help attract these birds. Martins will return to the same nesting site year after year, as long as there are no structures or trees within 40 feet of the nest box pole on all sides.

First, your nest box needs to be in a habitat in which your target bird is comfortable. If you have a large lot with some dense stands of trees, you'll have better luck attracting black-capped chickadees than you would in an open field—and your odds improve if you stuff the nest box with wood shavings and sawdust, so the bird can excavate its own cavity. If you live on the edge of a wide meadow, eastern bluebirds or tree swallows may come to your nest box, especially if it's fastened to the post in a split-rail fence.

Box height is a large factor for certain species. Northern flicker, eastern screech owl, and American kestrel all prefer higher nests, as much as 30 feet off the ground. Many small birds, including Carolina wren, prothonotary warbler, red-breasted nuthatch, and tufted titmouse, are comfortable in nest boxes from 5 to 15 feet off the ground. Bluebirds and house wrens look for lower nest boxes, with wrens topping out at 10 feet and bluebirds choosing to be 3 to 6 feet up.

Birdhouse with a 1½-inch-size hole

Many birds establish an area in which only one mated pair can nest. This is the birds' territory, and birds will defend that area from all other birds of its species that might approach. Kestrels, for example, will not nest within half a mile of one another. Even little chickadees establish significant territory, permitting one nest in an area of several acres. Once birds choose your nest box, your yard becomes their territory, and they will defend the area—sometimes aggressively—against avian intruders.

INTRUDERS

It's lovely to consider the possibility of nuthatches, titmice, or bluebirds nesting in your yard . . . but the fact is that aggressive invasive species may be the first to find the boxes you've placed for more desirable birds. House

Preferred Entrance Hole Sizes

House wren	1 to 1¼ inches
Chickadee	1⅛ inches
Titmouse	1¼ inches
Downy woodpecker	1¼ inches
Nuthatch	1⅜ inches
Carolina wren	1½ inches
Bluebird	1½ inches
Tree swallow	1½ inches
Hairy woodpecker	1¾ inches
Purple martin	2¼ inches
Flicker	2½ inches

sparrows and European starlings are invasive species, introduced to our skies and woods by well-meaning Americans in the mid to late 1800s.

As invaders, they had no natural predators, so their numbers multiplied with exponential speed. Today these two species are among the most populous in the United States—in part because they can nest and breed just about anywhere, including in nest boxes meant for other birds.

House sparrows are particularly partial to blue-bird boxes. Many birders have observed house sparrows actively pushing bluebirds out of nest boxes—actually killing their nestlings. Starlings also kill bluebirds; if that's not reason enough to discourage them, they also are noisy, they roost in huge flocks, they devour your seed and chase away smaller birds, and they leave their droppings all over your property.

As house sparrows and starlings are not native to the United States, the Federal Migratory Bird Treaty Act of 1918 does not protect them, so we are within our rights to discourage their nesting behavior. That being said, it may feel squeamish to remove starling or house sparrow nesting material and even their

A brown-headed cowbird laid an egg in this Carolina wren nest, leaving her baby for the wren to raise.

eggs from your nest boxes. The fact is that one removal may not be enough: House sparrows raise up to four broods per season, so you may find yourself with another nest to deal with just weeks after you've dispensed with the first.

In the end, the only way to defeat the birds may be to take down your nest boxes. Even this is a small step, however, as house sparrows will nest just about anywhere: in your rain gutters, in signs at retail stores, or in a hole in your garage or eaves.

House sparrows consider nesting in a hole over a garage.

Beyond sparrows and starlings, there are more insidious dangers to nesting songbirds. Brown-headed cowbirds are "brood parasites," laying their eggs in other birds' nests and leaving the other birds to incubate and raise their young. Often, the cowbird nestling is born first and is many times the size of a bird's other offspring—as you can see on page 115, in comparison to a Carolina wren nestling. The baby cowbird's aggressive feeding behavior may starve the other nestlings. What you do with a cowbird egg is your business, but remember that it is illegal for humans to remove a cowbird egg from another bird's nest.

NEST BOX MAINTENANCE

Most birds build a new nest every year—or several, as they raise more than one brood each season, and each clutch gets a fresh nest. The nests from the previous season or brood may seem like keepsakes or teaching tools for your children, but the fact is that they can become havens for parasites, lice, and mites. Equally important, the droppings and other leavings in the nest can be harmful to humans if we inhale the dust from these materials.

Once the nestlings have fledged, the birds abandon the nest. It's time for you to clean out the nest box, making it ready for the next breeding birds to consider it as a nesting site.

Start by assembling the tools you'll need to clear the nesting material and other detritus from the box. You'll need a pair of nonporous gloves, an ice scraper or other tool with a sharp blade for scraping, and a thick plastic trash bag.

NATURAL NEST MATERIAL

You don't need to hang up a variety of nest boxes to invite birds to nest in and around your yard.

Birds have been nesting without our help for millions of years, and most species prefer trees, bushes, natural cavities, and crevices in man-made structures to the boxes we craft so carefully.

What nearly every nesting bird needs is suitable material with which to build a sturdy nest. The shape, size, and construction of the nest varies with each bird species: some appear to be a haphazard pile of loose sticks, while others are intricately woven baskets lined with petal-soft feathers, leaves, or even pussy willows. Your yard can be a treasure trove of supplies for busy builders.

It takes weeks for a bird to complete the nest construction process for each brood, so you'll see birds gathering nesting material throughout the spring and summer, first building the firm foundation that will hold the nest in place, and then creating the armature to cradle the eggs. The last step is the nest lining, ingeniously designed to be moisture resistant, to help keep the eggs warm, and to create a soft seat for the incubating mother.

How can your yard and garden assist in the nest-building process? Your trees, shrubs, and flowers can produce many of the essentials for strong, sturdy nests.

- **Brush Pile.** Resist the urge to rake and bag up every fallen leaf and errant twig from your yard, as these are integral elements of a good nest. Instead, make a brush pile by raking together fallen or pruned branches and twigs. Choose a corner of your yard in

HOW TO CLEAN A NESTING BOX EFFECTIVELY

Step 1: What's in There?

First, put on your gloves. Open the nest box and see what's inside. Usually, you'll find a nest made from any number of materials: twigs, string, grass, leaves, bits of paper or cloth, yarn, or even spider webs or cocoons.

You may see eggshells as well. It's also possible you'll find a dead nestling.

Step 2: Clear the Nest

Remove the nest with your gloved hand, and drop the nest into your bag. You may have some scraping to do to get the guano (droppings) off the cavity walls and floor. If the guano is hardened, use a spray

bottle to wet it down. This will help make it soft. Scrape all the material out and directly into your bag. Be very careful not to breathe in any of the dust from this material.

Step 3: Disinfecting

Once the nest box is cleaned out, disinfect it with a mix of one part bleach to nine parts water. Use a spray bottle to apply the water/bleach mix to the inside walls of the box. Don't use any commercial disinfectants, flea powders, or insecticides! These are very bad for the birds. The bleach/water solution is enough to kill any remaining blowflies or parasites. Let the box dry completely.

Step 4: Good Things to Know

If you find an unhatched egg inside the box, you may be tempted to keep it. The egg may be rotten, however, as the fetus inside either did not develop at all, or died before it could hatch. Even if the egg seems harmless, it's a breeding ground for viruses like E. coli and streptococcus. If the infertile egg breaks, it can spread these viruses. The best thing to do is discard the egg.

Once you've cleaned the box thoroughly, winterize it for roosting birds by placing a piece of cardboard in the bottom. This will block the drainage holes, which will help keep the wind from blowing in. Place dried grasses inside, to help roosting birds keep warm through the winter.

which you can leave these limbs permanently. When you prune your trees or shrubs, add more to the pile. Birds will use bits of the pile for nesting material—and perhaps even nest within it.

- **Last Year's Leaves.** Leaves often collect under shrubs and trees. It's customary to rake and bag them, but if we let them be, birds will use some of them as nest lining. When you clear last year's leaves from your yard in spring, leave some piles under your shrubs. Even beyond nesting, ground-feeding birds forage under leaves for grubs and insects, so you may draw more thrushes and wrens to your yard. The added bonus: The leaves will decompose and serve as natural mulch.

- **Grasses.** How do birds make their nests so strong? Some use long, supple grasses to weave the twigs together in a basket shape. Add native grasses to your landscape, allowing them to grow naturally high in summer and die back in the fall and winter. Birds will gather the long, dry blades and "sew" them into their nests.

- **Mud.** Birds have an instinctive understanding of the need to make their nests as waterproof and solid as possible. One of the ways they accomplish this is with mud. You may see birds struggling to fly with pats of mud in their bills, a sure sign that a nest is coming together and is ready for its lining. Mud may be available along the edge of the pond you've installed, or under your birdbath. Let it be through the spring and summer, to give birds the water-resistant mortar they need.

WHEN BIRDS NEST

If house wrens started building nests in your boxes last year on April 15, can you expect them to do so at about the same time this year?

The simple answer is that there's no simple answer. Birds' breeding schedules can be as disparate as the number of sunny days you have in one spring versus the next.

These house wrens have chosen their nest box.

The birds themselves will provide plenty of clues to their nesting plans. Resident birds from jays to house sparrows take on brighter mantles as the mating season approaches. Goldfinches slough off their dull winter feathers as bright lemon-yellow growth replaces them. Soon males of every species bicker and peck at one another at feeders and on branches as they establish territories.

Many birds mate for life, including house finches. Even the mated pairs exhibit courtship behavior as a precursor to breeding, however, so you are likely to see some interesting goings-on at your feeders. If you see a male house finch feeding a female, you're witnessing courtship. The female actively solicits food from the male, and the male offers her food and actually feeds her. He may continue to do this for weeks, right through the incubation of the eggs.

Other signs of courtship include males and females chasing one another around your yard and puffed-up male birds on a twig or feeder showing off their fine features to attract mates. Soon you may witness actual mating, as the male bird mounts the female. Fertilized eggs will not be far behind.

Two northern flickers in a courtship ritual

April and May are prime nesting months for a first brood, with most of the activity well underway by the second to third week of May. However, harsh weather conditions and lasting cold spells can slow progress, holding migratory birds back from their accustomed breeding grounds.

Nest siting can begin as early as March: Non-migratory male and female pairs may begin shopping around for an appropriate cavity or branch. Birds may roost throughout the winter in any number of holes and openings throughout your neighborhood, but a mated pair is most likely scouting for a spot to build the first nest of the season. If the birds show an interest in a spot they should not, now is the time to seal a crack, mend a screen, or cover a hole in your garage or barn.

Hawks and owls in your neighborhood may accelerate the breeding schedule, starting earlier than smaller species. Most of these larger birds do not build nests of their own, using nests abandoned by other birds, cavities excavated by woodpeckers, or larger nest boxes you provide. Watch for these birds in late February and March, with breeding extending into late April and May.

Some birds—American robins and house wrens in particular—will build several nests at the outset. The birds then choose one nest from these and the female lays her eggs in that one. If you find a line of nests on a beam or branch, they may be the work of robins. House wrens often build nests in several different nest boxes. They will choose just one for their first clutch, but the male house wren will continue to defend the other nests, chattering and behaving aggressively toward any birds that approach.

WHERE BIRDS NEST

Whether your have a wooded lot with evergreen or leafy trees, an open meadow filled with nodding wildflowers, or a city yard with houses just past the driveways on either side, birds can find places to nest on your property and nearby.

Most birds choose the crotch of a tree or a strong branch higher up on which to build a nest—but many birds pass up trees in favor of depressions in the ground, a convenient "shelf" created by a roof beam, or a sheltered spot under an arbor, bridge, or viaduct.

It seems like it would be fairly easy to find a bird's nest, but here's where the birds are smarter than we might realize. Birds use natural nesting material like grass, leaves, and lichens to camouflage their nests, making them virtually indistinguishable from the surrounding foliage. You may have a bird's nest nearly in front of your face against the trunk of a pine tree, but the nest may be brilliantly covered by bits of pine needles and twigs, truly hiding it in plain sight.

Not all birds are so crafty, however. The birds in your yard may find their way into your hanging planters, a corner of your garage or porch, a portal created by vines curling around your patio railings, or a cozy spot inside an outdoor lighting fixture.

Birds use natural materials to build their nests.

The best way to locate a nest is to watch the birds from a distance, using your binoculars or scope, to determine if they regularly enter and leave the same tree, shrub, or other shelter. Birds repeatedly entering the same bush at the same spot may very well be building a nest there. By the same token, birds spotted slipping through a hole in your garage again and again are undoubtedly in the construction business.

- **Tree Nesters.** Thanks in part to dozens of cartoons and children's picture books, most of us assume that birds nest primarily in trees. Indeed, many of our backyard birds do choose trees, with American robins as the most common backyard tree nesters. Most songbirds (warblers, vireos, and the like) build cup nests in trees as well.

- **Cavity Nesters.** Woodpeckers, sapsuckers, nuthatches, chickadees, and flickers nest in tree cavities. They excavate these holes with their strong bills to make a large enough space for the female and a brood of nestlings. While some of these birds come back to the same cavity year after year, most move on to create a new hole. Check the old cavity anyway, because owls often use abandoned holes in trees for their own nests.

American robins often nest in dense bushes or trees.

- **Shelf Nesters.** Swallows and phoebes look for the combination of overhead shelter and surface stability, often building their nests inside man-made structures. If you see a nest on a roof beam or on top of a ledge in your garage, shed, or barn, chances are excellent that it's a barn swallow or phoebe nest. These birds may also choose the shelf-like curves of neon signs, beams under bridges, or holes that lead to the attic of your home.

- **Ground Nesters.** Some birds nest in the low branches of shrubs, or even right on the ground. Goldfinches and many sparrows prefer low nests, often choosing brush piles, the fallen branches of trees with needles, or the dense lower growth near a shrub's base. Your brush pile may be prime nesting habitat for white-crowned, white-throated, chipping or song sparrows, as well as dark-eyed juncos. Allowing some of your shrubs to keep their natural undergrowth—rather than pruning them to clear the lower story—can provide excellent nest sites for small birds.

NESTLINGS

Here's what happens once the birds finish their nest:

The female begins laying eggs, laying one every day until she's completed the clutch. How many eggs depends largely on the species: Mourning doves, for example, lay just two to three eggs in a clutch, while kinglets may lay anywhere from five to eleven eggs.

Incubation doesn't begin until all the eggs are laid, and then the female bird sits on the eggs until they hatch. Male birds often play a role in the incubation, taking over while the female forages for food.

For most backyard birds, incubation ends in twelve to fifteen days when the eggs hatch. Now all kinds of activity begins! If you listen closely, you're likely to hear the peeping of high voices begging for food. One or both parents are now busy with feeding, keeping their new brood satisfied while they see to their own needs as well. If you haven't spotted the nest itself by this time, watch for adult birds carrying food. Follow the bird with your binoculars to get an idea of where the nest and nestlings might be.

A barn swallow nestling makes his presence known.

Life is about eating, eating, eating for newborn chicks. The parents have more responsibilities than feeding their babies, however—they must also be careful not to give away the nest's location to predators. If you see a bird hopping to branches or other surfaces around its nest for several minutes before approaching, he or she is making certain that no hawks, cats, or other potential threats are watching before she darts in to feed the defenseless nestlings.

Parent birds forage far and wide for appropriate food to feed their nestlings. In some species, including western bluebirds, acorn woodpeckers, and American crows, cooperative groups form to care for the young. Even the previous year's offspring participate, until they reach maturity and begin nesting on their own. For most species, however, the mated pair—or often, the female alone—must maintain this constant feeding pace on its own.

Even birds that normally do not eat insects will feed them to their young. Insects provide the protein and other nutrition nestlings need to grow quickly and become strong. They also provide liquid, so there's no need for parents to bring water to the nest.

It's tempting to run up to a nest and peer inside, but your quick movements and proximity will agitate the parent, sending the adult away from the nest in the midst of incubating or feeding its young. You can observe the nest from a respectful, nonthreatening distance using a spotting scope.

FLEDGLINGS

How can you tell when the nestlings have made their first forays out of the nest and into the world?

It's easier than you think: They're full-grown but fuzzy-looking, their markings are not as bold or defined as their parents' plumage, and they seem to have Laurel and Hardy's aptitude for tumbling off of branches, bumping into one another and pecking ineffectively at feeders.

This American robin fledgling looks very different from its adult parents.

Most often, you'll discover the arrival of fledglings by glancing at your feeders and finding seven patchy-colored northern cardinals, for example, where there were just two throughout the spring. Keep watching the comings and goings in your yard and you'll see American robins with light-colored, speckled breasts, or dull gray starlings dazedly watching their parents feeding on the ground, occasionally poking with their bills in imitation of their parents' foraging behavior.

Fledglings often have not yet grown the longer tail feathers their parents sport, so their flying can be off-balance at first. Parent birds often feed their young, catching an insect and passing it on bill-to-bill to their offspring. You may see this process at your feeders, as the parents bring the fledglings to the food, demonstrate how to pick up seeds, and then drop the seeds from their own bills into the open mouths of their young. Eventually, the parents nudge the fledglings toward the food to encourage them to gather their own seed or suet.

The high-pitched squeaks you heard while the babies begged for food in the nest are now replaced by hoarse or rasping calls that can't approximate the parents' more melodious songs. In particular, immature American crows develop a rough, scratchy call that's not unlike a crow with laryngitis. Listen for new songs and calls that don't quite pass muster and you'll know that fledglings are nearby.

Birding Tip: Baby Bird 911

What should you do with a baby bird that's fallen out of its nest?

- If it has feathers and it can move around on its own, leave it where you found it. Many nestlings leave the nest before they fly; the parents may know where the bird is and may be feeding it regularly until it matures. This little bird is a fledgling; it will most likely be fine without your help.

- If the bird is too young to have feathers, look around and overhead for the nest. If it's within reach, place the bird back in the nest as quickly as possible. It's a myth that birds will smell human contact—your touching the nestling will not bother the parents.

- If the nest has been destroyed, your last option is to call the nearest animal shelter or bird rehabilitation center in your area. Trained professionals will know what action to take.

It's remarkable to watch these young birds change and grow over the course of a few days or weeks, as they gain agility, independence, and resourcefulness.

This blue jay easily dominates the house sparrow.

9 Tips for Bird Identification

Now that you've got your flowers, trees and feeders in place, it's time to understand what kinds of birds may arrive in your yard. This chapter will help you learn how to identify the most common birds in the New England states, particularly the ones that may pay a visit to your feeders.

In a field guide, birds look distinctly different from species to species. Arrows and call-outs help draw your attention to the distinguishing field marks, and multiple drawings or photos help you learn how to tell one bird from another.

In real life, with birds hopping behind leaves or standing directly between you and the sun, identification becomes much more complex. Brown, gray, and brightly colored birds swoop in and out of your field of vision, disappearing as quickly as they came.

Before your eyes cross, here's the number one rule for improving your bird identification skills: *Look at the bird before you look it up.*

Start with the bird's basic shape. Generally, the species in the same family of birds—warblers, vireos, doves, hawks, ducks, geese, and so on—have a similar, fairly recognizable shape from head to tail. It may take some time to learn these, but you will soon see that a sparrow has a short, heavy bill, while a wren has a longer, sharper bill. By the same token, the wren's tail stands perpendicular to its body, differentiating it from a sparrow, which has a long, usually fan-shaped tail.

Look at the bird's size. Warblers and vireos are smaller than sparrows, for example, and sparrows are smaller than towhees. If your bird is smaller than a robin but larger than a warbler, you know something about what kind of bird it may be. Bigger birds are easier to see, so you may learn the larger birds—robins, towhees, jays, phoebes, kingbirds and the like—faster than you will the smaller birds. Birds of the same family may differ slightly in size—a house wren, for example, is significantly smaller than a Carolina wren, and some warblers are larger than others. When you look from one bird to another in your backyard, however, you can make a size comparison in no time.

What is the bird doing? A bird creeping up the side of a tree may be a woodpecker, nuthatch, or brown creeper. A bird sorting through leaves on the ground is more likely a towhee, thrush, or sparrow than an oriole or flycatcher. Behavior can tell you enough about the bird to guess its family, even if its wing patterns or tail colors are obscured from your view.

FIELD MARKS

Ever since Roger Tory Peterson introduced the world to the concept of field marks in 1934, the process of identifying the bird in your binoculars became much easier. We owe much of bird watching's popularity to Peterson, who published the very first field guide. Captivated by birds in seventh grade, Peterson developed a passion for identifying species, sketching birds in the field and noting the characteristics he called "field marks." When his first book sold out its entire printing in two weeks, modern birding was born . . . and today, tens of millions of birders around the

Goldfinches and house finches are both in the finch family.

world rely on field marks for bird identification.

Today, field marks are one of the many tools we can use to gain confidence in our ability to tell one bird species from another.

The concept is simple: Look at as many of the bird's markings as you can in the time you see the bird. Each part of the bird becomes important: head, chest, wings, tail, underbody, and feet. Ornithologists and hard-core birders divide each of these parts into dozens of subsections with names like supraloral, tibial feathers, malar, and coverts, but we'll start here with the basics.

Here's the most important advice we can give you: Look at all the field marks, not just one or two. Many woodpeckers have red on the backs of their heads, for example, but only a couple of these have black and white horizontal stripes running from their shoulders all the way down their backs. One field mark is rarely enough to identify any bird species, but a collection of observations—along with the bird's size, shape, behavior, diet, habitat, and range—will help you narrow down the possibilities.

Field marks are a terrific identification tool, but they are just one tool in your bird identification kit. Use them all to learn what new arrival has found its way to your yard.

MIGRATION PATTERNS

The movement of millions of birds across the continents twice a year comes as seasons change, often beginning well before the weather has turned warmer or colder. Birds respond instinctively to factors beyond temperature. They react to the length of days and the angle of natural light as the earth's Northern Hemisphere tilts toward the sun in spring, and begins to pull back from the sun in late summer and fall. The result is a regularly changing pageant at your feeders and in your trees and shrubs, bringing an assortment of birds that spend the warmer months in North America.

Birds habitually return to the same general breeding grounds from year to year, so you are likely to see the same birds at your feeders—many of which remember exactly where you placed the food the year before. New birds will come as well, including some species you may not have seen in previous years.

As you riffle through your field guide to find the new bird, how can you narrow down the search?

Just about every field guide provides a map of North America on the page with the photos or illustrations of

A Baltimore oriole arrives at a familiar feeder in spring.

the birds. This map is color-coded to help you understand where the bird lives at different times of the year, where the species nests and breeds, and where occasional or rare individuals have popped up unexpectedly.

It's important to understand that not every species can be seen all over America. In fact, only a tiny fraction of the continent's 900-plus bird species live in every state and province.

Knowing which birds live in your area year-round, which ones migrate through in spring and fall, and which ones nest in your region will help you identify new species more quickly.

HABITAT

While people can adapt to just about any environment by building high-tech protective shelters and augmenting our clothing, most living things—especially

This common yellowthroat lives on the abundant supply of insects generated by wetlands, marshes, and waterfront areas.

birds—are adapted to specific environments. Birds need to live in the right habitat to thrive, based on the foods they eat, the kind of shelter they know how to construct, and the amount of water they require to maintain their own health.

In New England, wetlands attract water-loving birds like long-legged waders, shorebirds, ducks, and geese. Open meadows are perfect for upland game birds and foraging blackbirds and hawks. Forests are homes to dozens of cavity-nesting species that devour the insects they find under tree bark and in the air, making the most of the trees as sturdy, reliable shelter.

As you consider the birds you'd like to attract to your backyard, take into consideration the habitat that surrounds you and your home. No matter how many wood duck houses you put up in your suburban subdivision, for example, you won't get a single one of these water-loving birds if there's no sizeable, secluded pond in your area. If your home is surrounded by dense forest, you're not likely to see grassland birds like meadowlarks and savannah sparrows.

Focus on birds that are native to your habitat, and you'll have far more luck in attracting these birds to your yard.

MALE AND FEMALE PLUMAGE

Everyone loves to see brightly colored birds in the backyard, so there's considerable excitement when an American goldfinch, purple finch, or Baltimore oriole arrives at the feeder. As you watch these gorgeous birds, however, you may see that they bring their gray, brown, or olive friends that are not so pleasing to the eye.

In most bird species, the males have showy, well-defined markings in bold or bright colors, and some go so far as to produce an iridescent shimmer in the sun. Their ornamental tones have one specific purpose: Female birds are attracted to the flashiest males. The brighter and more defined the male's colors, the more interesting he will be to a potential mate.

Producing all that color takes energy, especially for birds with spectacular tails or crests. If you've ever seen a displaying wild turkey, with his fanlike tail unfurled and his head turned bright blue, you know that some significant exertion is involved to create these effects. Most birds expend many calories producing their spring coats, so they eat more—making your feeders the hot spots for male activity and female observation.

Female birds also require the camouflage to stay out of sight while they sit on their nests for weeks at a

Female northern cardinal **Male northern cardinal**

stretch in spring and summer. In fall, when birds begin the migration southward, many of the males lose their pretty colors and turn nearly as drab as their mates. This strategy helps them hide from predators as they rest and feed during the long flight to warmer climates.

SEASONAL PLUMAGE

Once the breeding season ends, you may notice that the male birds in your backyard start to look a little less flashy and vibrant.

Many beginning birders become concerned when they spot a goldfinch that appears to be molting. The bird may still bear much of his lemon-yellow coloration, but patches of color have given way, revealing olive brown areas that look as though the bird might be ill.

There's no need for concern—these birds are healthy and are going through a very normal process. Over the summer months, birds' flamboyant feathers wear away, and are replaced with a more practical layer of earth-toned colors. These provide the disguise birds need to blend in seamlessly with brush piles, leafless tree branches, and shrubbery as they make their trip south to their overwintering grounds.

Seeing the birds change their colors in late summer and early fall signals the approaching cooler seasons, often long before the leaves of deciduous trees transform to their spectacular fall tones.

Downy woodpecker female

10 The Birds in Your Garden

This quick reference guide will help you determine which birds have arrived in your garden. The birds included here are common to backyards, fields, and forests throughout the New England states. Your own neighborhood may attract some additional species, especially if you live near water or on the edge of a significant wetland. When the bird in your garden is not pictured in this book, turn to your favorite field guide for additional options.

SMALL BIRDS

These common birds are likely to build nests in areas they share with people, and they're just as likely to scold you loudly if you come too close to their nest site. Watch for fledglings at your feeders by mid to late May, as the parent birds teach their young to become the next generation of feeder birds in your yard.

Chickadees and goldfinches can perch or cling to your feeders, as they are just as comfortable feeding in a vertical position as they are standing upright. Song and chipping sparrows may feed voraciously on seeds in the winter, and then switch to insects and grubs when they become plentiful in summer.

American goldfinch

The only bird in North America with an all-yellow body and black wings, the male goldfinch is one of our easiest birds to spot. The female has a grayish mantle and streaky sides, with a yellow wash over her breast and throat.

American goldfinch

Habitat: Open fields, orchards, suburban and rural backyards.

Food: Very partial to nyjer seeds and sunflower hearts; also some insects.

Nest: In the fork of a horizontal tree branch. The female incubates the eggs; they usually hatch in twelve to fourteen days.

Black-capped chickadee

Each quadrant of the United States has its own chickadee species, but these cheeky little birds call more than half of the country and Canada their home. The male and female are identical.

Black-capped chickadee

Habitat: Any area with a lot of trees, including neighborhoods in any environment.

Food: Sunflower and safflower seeds, peanuts, suet.

Nest: Chickadees are cavity nesters that excavate their own holes. They will use nest boxes stuffed with wood shavings or sawdust, allowing them to dig their own cavity. The eggs hatch in twelve to fifteen days.

Chipping sparrow

Smaller than a house sparrow with a rusty cap and clear breast, this little bird arrives in flocks and stays throughout the season. The male and female are identical; they migrate to the northeastern states in spring.

Habitat: Suburban neighborhoods and any other buildings with lawns.

Food: Sunflower and safflower seeds, mixed seed blends. These birds will perch on feeders, but they prefer the ground.

Chipping sparrow

Nest: Usually in pine trees or other conifers, 3 to 10 feet off the ground. The female incubates, and the male joins her to feed the nestlings. Eggs hatch in eleven to fourteen days.

Song sparrow

You'll hear this bird's jubilant song before you see one. A small sparrow with a streaky breast and a big black dot in the center of its chest, song sparrows can vary from dark brown to a reddish shade.

Habitat: Suburban yards, in vegetation near water, farm fields.

Food: Sunflower and safflower seeds, mixed seed blends. These birds will perch on feeders, but they prefer the ground.

Song sparrow

Nest: On the ground, often in a brush pile or under a bush. The female incubates, and the eggs hatch in twelve to thirteen days.

American tree sparrow

A winter visitor to most of the United States, this little sparrow nests in northern Canada. The black dot in the middle of a clear breast, coupled with the rusty cap, make this an easy bird to pick out from a winter sparrow flock.

Habitat: Shrubby areas, woods with brushy edges, frozen swamps in winter, tundra in summer.

Food: Naturally occurring seeds; these sparrows will come to feeders as well.

American tree sparrow

Nest: In a natural depression on the ground or just off the ground in a low shrub; incubation takes twelve to fifteen days.

House sparrow

Familiar because of their ability to find new feeders before any other birds do, house sparrows dominate the cities and suburbs. The male's black bib and gray and rufous cap differentiate him from the more drably marked female.

Habitat: Cities, suburbs, and anywhere where people congregate.

Food: Seeds and suet from feeders; table scraps and crumbs left by humans.

Nest: In a store sign, on a window ledge or beam, inside an open pipe, or in any other man-made structure.

House sparrow

House finch

With its bright red (or sometimes orange) face and streaky sides, the male house finch brings welcome color to a winter feeder. The female's streaky breast and sides make her easy to spot; finches usually forage in pairs.

Habitat: Woods and other areas with lots of foliage, suburban yards and parks.

Food: Seeds and suet from feeders; seeds found in the wild.

House finch

Nest: Nest boxes, tree cavities, in small sheltered places near human structures (inside an outdoor light fixture, in a hanging planter).

Pine siskin

This streaky bird looks like a cross between a sparrow and a finch, and is actually part of the finch family. Longer-billed than a sparrow, the siskin male has light yellow wing bars that help you name this species at a glance. Siskins winter in the northeastern states.

Habitat: Pine forests, as its name would suggest, and backyards near forested areas.

Food: Seeds are the staple, making the siskin a regular visitor to feeders.

Pine siskin

Nest: Siskins nest in scattered colonies on the branches of coniferous trees. Incubation begins when the first egg is laid, and first hatching occurs after thirteen days.

House wren

If it seems like all of your nest boxes are filling up with twigs and grass but you don't see any birds inside, you've probably got a pair of house wrens. The tiny, loquacious males build several nests to impress a mate, who chooses just one for her brood. Look for a brown or grayish bird with a striped tail held upright and a long, slightly sloping bill.

Habitat: Wood edges, shrubs and brush piles, as well as dense bushes in gardens; you'll hear the house wren's raucous song long before seeing one.

Food: Exclusively insects, from beetles to spiders.

Nest: Busy cavity nesters, building a cup nest in a wren house (with a 1⅛-inch entrance hole). Nestlings hatch in fifteen to seventeen days.

House wren

Ruby-crowned kinglet

Tiny, greenish, and moving every second, kinglets are even more frenetic than most warblers. Watch for the tiny cream-colored eye ring, the bright white wing bar, and the raised, bright red crest on the male kinglet.

Habitat: High in trees and down in low shrubs in wooded areas.

Food: Gnats and other tiny insects.

Nest: Usually in spruce trees or other conifers with dense needles; the nest can be as much as 100 feet off the ground. Eggs hatch in about two weeks.

Ruby-crowned kinglet

Ruby-throated hummingbird

The most dependable (and usually the only) humming-bird at your feeders is this beautiful species. Once you see the male's jewel-like gorget light up in the sun, you'll know exactly what bird you have. The female ruby-throat tends to be a bright green with some golden highlights. She's dull gray to white in front.

Habitat: Wooded areas and backyards with trees.

Food: Plant nectar, tiny insects, and sugar water from feeders.

Nest: A tiny cup on top of a tree branch; incubation takes twelve to fourteen days.

Ruby-throated hummingbird

Purple finch

Washed with pink as if the bird has bathed in raspberry juice, the purple finch is not as common as the closely related house finch, but its voice and habits are essentially the same. The purple finch lacks the streaky sides of the house finch, but the female makes up for this with bolder, darker breast streaks and a bright white eyebrow.

Purple finch

Habitat: Areas with many trees and shrubs.

Food: Naturally occurring seeds including maple, ash, sycamore, and weeds, as well as some berries and insects.

Nest: In a conifer with dense needles, often as much as 60 feet off the ground. The female incubates the eggs, which hatch in about thirteen days.

Carolina wren

This large wren announces itself loudly with its "teakettle-teakettle-teakettle" call. Watch for its quick movements, straight-up tail, and bright white eyebrow stripe.

Habitat: Woods, parks, marshes, areas with lots of shrubs, and neighborhoods. This wren's range has expanded northward into some areas of New England.

Food: Strictly an insectivore.

Carolina wren

Nest: A dense cup that seems to lean on its side, often found in hanging plants, flowerpots, and other small, sheltered places.

Tufted titmouse

Small and sleek, this little gray-mantled bird displays rosy flanks, a black eye and forehead, and a white chest and face.

Habitat: Wooded areas with broadleaf trees, including parks, orchards, and neighborhoods. Titmice prefer elevations below 2,000 feet.

Food: Bugs, spiders, and snails, as well as berries, nuts, and seeds.

Nest: Natural or previously excavated holes in trees, in

Tufted titmouse

which they build cup-shaped nests. Titmice also use nest boxes.

LARGER PERCHING BIRDS

Not all of these birds will frequent your feeders, but you will know that they are in your yard when you hear their songs. Some may stop at your platform feeder—especially if you're feeding with raisins or other small fruits—for an energy pick-me-up as they migrate to their breeding grounds.

Insects and invertebrates play a critical role in attracting these birds to your yard. Mockingbirds, red-winged blackbirds, catbirds, kingbirds and phoebes catch flying insects, while robins pull worms and grubs out of the ground. Blackbirds have expanded their range significantly because they are opportunistic feeders, plundering farmers' fields for corn left behind after the harvest or snacking on millet at your feeders.

Robins' nests are the most common nests to find in your backyard or near your home. These birds prefer to nest on a shelf of some kind—a flat surface like a roof beam, a corner under your porch ceiling, at the top of a trellis, or anywhere else that offers a stable support.

They may be harder to find, but you may come across a mockingbird or catbird nest in your yard. Both of these species choose tall shrubs for nesting, and catbirds have shown a preference for bushes in suburban gardens.

Red-winged blackbirds are secretive nesters, hiding their nests in masses of last year's reeds and cattails in marshes or at the edges of ponds.

Gray catbird

Named for its mewing call that sounds eerily like a cat, this velvet-gray bird wears a showy black cap and flashes

Gray catbird

ruddy undertail coverts. You may see a lot of gray birds in your yard, but this is the only one with a black cap.

Habitat: In shady, wooded areas, particularly along hedgerows and among large shrubs.

Food: Catbirds eat insects and invertebrates, and have a special taste for Japanese beetles. Berries are also on the menu.

Nest: Catbirds nest deep in a bush 3–10 feet from the ground. The eggs hatch in twelve to thirteen days.

Northern mockingbird

The mockingbird's rapid-fire series of disparate calls often confuses new birders; this bird can have as many as fifty different melodies in its repertoire. An all-gray bird with a long tail that points upward when it perches, the mockingbird flashes large white wing and tail patches when it flies, making it particularly easy to identify.

Habitat: Suburban areas with lots of trees and shrubs, as well as city parks.

Food: Mockingbirds eat insects and love fruit, often defending a berry-laden tree from all comers for hours at a time.

Northern mockingbird

Nest: Look in trees and shrubs, or even in thick masses of vines between 3 and 10 feet from the ground. The eggs hatch in twelve to thirteen days.

American robin

The harbinger of spring across the northern states, the robin can be found in every state and is one of America's most widely recognized birds. You'll see them scattered across mowed lawns, cocking their heads and listening for earthworms moving just below the surface.

American robin

Habitat: Cities and suburbs, parks and wooded areas.

Food: Invertebrates are the favorite, but robins eat berries in winter. They may come to mealworm feeders.

Nest: Often on ledges or beams of buildings, or in the crotch of a tree. Eggs hatch in twelve to fourteen days.

Red-winged blackbird

A migrating bird that is one of the first to appear in New England as spring arrives, this bird's flashy red and yellow epaulets make it a perennial favorite. Its "onk-or-REEE" call signals the beginning of warmer weather.

Habitat: Any area with water and brushy or tall grasses and reeds.

Food: Seeds and invertebrates; the red-winged readily comes to feeders until grubs and bugs are available.

Red-winged blackbird

Nest: Low in bunches of reeds, sedge, grasses, or other tall vegetation, often in colonies. The eggs hatch in ten to twelve days.

Eastern meadowlark

If you're fortunate enough to live near an open meadow, or even if you have a large property with some acreage you allow to grow without mowing, you may attract meadowlarks to your extended backyard.

Habitat: Open, unmowed fields, prairies and meadows, cultivated fields with tall crops.

Food: Insects, worms, and natural seeds or those left from harvested crops.

Nest: In a depression on the ground, lined with grasses and horsehair. Incubation lasts thirteen to fourteen days.

Eastern meadowlark

Northern cardinal

The only all-red bird in the eastern states, the cardinal's bright color, tall crest, and black face are unmistakable. The female's soft brown mantle, red-edged wings and tail, and bright orange bill make her equally easy to identify.

Habitat: Woods, dense shrubs, tall trees, thickets, and other areas that offer concentrated cover and high perches.

Food: Sunflower and other seeds, berries, fruit on trees, and occasional insects.

Nest: An elaborate cup with several layers of material, usually in the middle of a dense shrub. Incubation takes eleven to thirteen days.

Northern cardinal

Blue jay

The most prevalent jay east of the Mississippi River, this bold, aggressive bird can dominate a feeder. Nonetheless,

Blue jay

its intricate color patterns, sharp crest, and bold facial markings make it a backyard favorite. Listen for the jay's gurgling alternate call, one that confuses many a beginning birder.

Habitat: Forests, particularly around the edges.

Food: Jays are particularly fond of acorns. They forage for seeds, nuts, and insects from trees, and come to feeders for sunflower seeds. They are also known to eat eggs and nestlings from smaller birds' nests.

Nest: A mass of entwined twigs in the crotch or branches of a tall tree. It takes seventeen to eighteen days for the eggs to hatch.

Rose-breasted grosbeak

Easy to spot with its vivid magenta breast, white front, black head and startlingly large gray-white bill (the "gross beak"), the grosbeak arrives in the states in late April to early May. You may not recognize his mate, a streaky brown-and-white bird easily mistaken for a big finch or a female red-winged blackbird.

Habitat: Forests of mixed deciduous and coniferous trees, young woods and parks, on the edges of moist areas, and in suburbs with mature trees.

Food: Seeds and fruit at feeders, as well as insects.

Nest: In a leafy tree or shrub with dense foliage. The nests tend to be loosely constructed—you may see the eggs right through the bottom. Incubation takes twelve to fourteen days.

Rose-breasted grosbeak

Baltimore oriole

What could be easier to see than a bright orange bird with black head and wings? This stunning creature announces itself with a syrupy song that crosses the robin's warble with a cardinal's clear notes. The female's head is more shaded than solid black, and she wears a less vibrant shade of orange.

Baltimore oriole

Habitat: Open areas with clusters of leafy trees, neighborhoods with mature trees, and woodland edges.

Food: Orange halves, nectar, and grape jelly at your feeders, as well as insects, caterpillars, and fruit on trees.

Nest: Famously sack-shaped, carefully fastened to a supportive angle in a tree branch. Eggs hatch in eleven to fourteen days.

Orchard oriole

More of a burnt orange shade than its brighter counterparts, the orchard oriole is otherwise marked very much like a Baltimore oriole—but it's at least an inch shorter in length. Females are yellow with gray wings.

Habitat: In woods near streambeds, and near open fields and parks.

Food: Insects and spiders provide protein, while nectar and jelly from feeders give the bird its energy.

Orchard oriole

Nest: A suspended cup much like the Baltimore's, but not as long or deep. Incubation lasts about twelve to fourteen days.

Eastern kingbird

Solidly gray on top with a white cheek, chest, and underbelly, the eastern kingbird sports white tips at the end of its dark tail feathers, an easy field mark to spot when the bird flies.

Eastern kingbird

Habitat: Open fields, grasslands, and the edges of wooded areas.

Food: Insects caught in midair by flycatching.

Nest: On a sturdy tree limb or in the crotch of a tree. Incubation takes twelve to thirteen days, but the kingbird raises only one brood per season, caring for the young for nearly two months.

Eastern bluebird

With its blue head, wings, and back, and its orange breast and throat, the bluebird differentiates itself from the indigo bunting or blue jay with ease. Watch for one on a fence post or overhead on a wire. Females are grayish with blue highlights.

Habitat: Open fields, pastures, farmland, and marshes. Look for them at your local golf course.

Food: Crawling insects including larvae, caterpillars, and mealworms are favorites. Overwintering birds eat all kinds of berries.

Nest: If no nest box is suitable, bluebirds nest in cavities in trees high off the ground. Eggs hatch in eleven to nineteen days.

Eastern bluebird

Eastern phoebe

It's surprisingly easy to differentiate this bird from the rest of the flycatcher family: The phoebe is larger, with a darker head and tail, and it bobs its tail continuously. Listen for its scratchy "PHEE-bee" call.

Habitat: Open areas including the edges of fields, forests, and hedgerows.

Food: Watch the phoebe catch flies in midair—these are its staple diet.

Eastern phoebe

Nest: Check your garage, shed, or other outbuildings for nests close to the ceiling, on a beam or shelf. Eggs incubate for about sixteen days.

Purple martin

The largest member of the swallow family, this distinctly purple bird has a heavier chest, larger head, and longer body than most swallows. Females have grayish underparts and appear more blue than purple.

Habitat: Along the edges of large bodies of water, usually seen in flight.

Food: Martins fly over water to catch insects in midair.

Nest: Famous for their colony nesting behavior, martins nest almost exclusively in multi-hole houses provided by humans. The house must be placed near water. Incubation takes fifteen to seventeen days.

Purple martin

TREE-CLINGING BIRDS

Birds that travel up and down the sides of trees remain a novelty even after you've seen thousands of them. The fact that these birds are comfortable hanging by their feet from the underside of a branch makes them a marvel as well as a curiosity.

The prerequisite for attracting these birds is a stand of trees, particularly aspen or poplars that become hollow as they decay from the inside. Nuthatches prefer dead trees, either with natural cavities of their own or with holes previously excavated by woodpeckers.

If you see a lot of woodpecker activity in your area and you can't spot the nesting cavity, try looking at the undersides of the largest tree branches. Downy woodpeckers often excavate a hole in this position, shielding the inside from spring rain while hiding the opening from predators.

Generally, our most common woodpeckers do not use nest boxes except to roost in winter. White-breasted nuthatches may choose a nest box, presumably if no suitable excavated cavity can be found.

One of the tricky things about attracting woodpeckers to your yard is their propensity for drumming a rhythm on buildings and wooden structures. Drumming is a territorial behavior, letting all the other woodpeckers in the vicinity know that this individual claims this area as his breeding ground. The birds often choose their drumming sites based on how loud their pounding sounds—so you may hear persistent tap-tap-tapping on your metal storm drain or chimney cap. In the worst cases, the bird can actually drill holes in your wood siding.

Downy woodpecker

America's smallest woodpecker, the downy's squeaky call often announces its approach—but it's the white stripe down the center of its back that makes it easy to identify. The male sports a bright red patch on the back of its head, while the female is virtually identical except for the lack of a red patch.

Habitat: Wooded areas, neighborhoods with trees, riparian areas.

Food: Insects found under the bark of trees, nuts and suet from feeders.

Nest: In a cavity it excavates in a tree or stump, or in a fence post or other tall wooden pole. Male and female share the incubation; birds hatch in twelve days.

Downy woodpecker

Hairy woodpecker

Nearly identical to the downy woodpecker, but larger and with a bill twice as long, the hairy woodpecker prefers mature woods for foraging and nesting. These woodpeckers occupy a territory for life, so you will see the same bird in every season.

Habitat: Wooded areas, neighborhoods with mature trees.

Food: Insects found in live trees, sunflower seeds, peanut butter, and raw suet.

Nest: In a cavity it excavates in a live or dead tree or stump. Male and female share the incubation; birds hatch in twelve days.

Hairy woodpecker

Red-breasted nuthatch

With its bright white eyebrow and sharp little bill, this tiny bird quickly catches your eye when it lands on your suet. It's most often seen in winter, but you may have a pair that comes to your yard year-round.

Habitat: Mixed woods, including evergreens and leafy trees.

Food: Sunflower seed, suet, insects, and peanuts.

Nest: In a dead tree cavity; the birds smear the entrance with wood resin (pitch) to keep out insects and other predators. Birds hatch in twelve days.

Red-breasted nuthatch

White-breasted nuthatch

You'll see this bird moving down the trunk of a tree upside-down and head first. Larger than the red-breasted nuthatch, this bird's bright white head and dapper black cap make it easy to spot against tree bark.

Habitat: Anywhere with mature trees.

White-breasted nuthatch

Food: Sunflower seed, suet, peanuts, insects.

Nest: This nuthatch will take advantage of an existing cavity, so you may find them in your nest box. Eggs hatch in twelve days.

Northern flicker

With its spotted breast, striped wings, and gray head—adorned with a red spot in males—flickers confuse many beginning birders. Look for the white rump as it flies.

Habitat: Open areas, including suburban lawns. You'll find flickers in woodland areas and parks as well.

Food: Ants and beetles are favorites; flickers dig in the ground for them.

Nest: In tree cavities that they excavate, sometimes returning to the cavity they used the year before. Eggs incubate for eleven to thirteen days.

Northern flicker

Red-bellied woodpecker

It's a bit of a mystery how this bird got its name, as its "red" belly is barely pinkish (though more visible in mating season). Its smooth tan breast and face make it unique in the eastern states.

Habitat: Wooded areas, including neighborhoods with mature trees.

Food: Insects are first on the menu, with nuts, pinecones, and fruit all tied for second. Seeds and suet supplement the bird's winter diet.

Nest: In tree cavities that they excavate, building the nest on the wood chips that remain in the hole. Eggs incubate for twelve days.

Red-bellied woodpecker

Pileated woodpecker

Pileated woodpecker

The largest woodpecker in New England, this bird's arrival feels like a special event. Watch for the all-dark body, the white underside of the wings, and a well-defined red crest on both the male and female.

Habitat: Wooded areas with large, mature trees.

Food: Partial to carpenter ants and other bugs that bore into wood. You may attract this bird with raw suet.

Nest: Pileated woodpeckers excavate large holes in living trees to find food, and do the same for nesting. Eggs hatch in about eighteen days.

Red-headed woodpecker

Red-headed woodpecker

The all-red head, white chest and blue-black wings make this bird easy to identify. You may discover a cache of insects or seeds stashed behind tree bark, stored by this woodpecker for later use.

Habitat: Areas with deciduous trees, whether an orchard, a stand of trees in an open field, or dead trees in a marsh.

Food: This bird eats everything: seeds, nuts, insects, berries, other birds' eggs, and small rodents.

Nest: In a hole in a dead tree, sometimes used repeatedly for a whole season. Eggs hatch in about fourteen days.

GROUND-FEEDING BIRDS

Many birds decline to perch on a feeder, choosing instead to keep both feet firmly underneath their bodies while they search for seeds or bugs on the ground or on a platform feeder.

Doves, cowbirds, and sparrows also will perch on a utility wire or clothesline while they survey the availability of food on the ground. Looking at birds on a wire is a great way to learn to distinguish birds by shape, as they become silhouetted against the bright sky.

The arrival of juncos on snow-covered lawns is a herald of winter's end, while the white-crowned and white-throated sparrow migration signals the beginning of the spring season. Mourning doves remain resident across the country throughout the year except in the northern Great Plains states, to which they return in spring.

Birders of all stripes share mixed feelings about the arrival of brown-headed cowbirds. These birds do not build nests of their own, but lay eggs in the nests of other birds—often rolling the other birds' eggs out of the nest to insert their own. Yellow warblers and song sparrows bear the brunt of these parasitic breeders—in many cases, birders discover multiple cowbird eggs in the nests of these much smaller birds. Some American robins and gray catbirds now recognize the dark, heavily speckled cowbird eggs as different from their own, and throw them out of their nests. Most birds, however, do their best to incubate the eggs and raise the young, even though the cowbird eggs and chicks are often several times the size of the birds' own. The result is devastating: The smaller nestlings perish while the young cowbird dominates, devouring all the food the parent birds provide.

The Migratory Bird Treaty Act of 1936 protects cowbirds, so it's against the law to remove cowbird eggs from other birds' nests.

European starling
Numerous and widespread, starlings dominate suburban roadsides and open fields, foraging in large, tight flocks

European starling

that seem to move in perfect synchronization. Thousands may appear in one place on utility and guide wires.

Habitat: Cities, suburbs, and anywhere people congregate.

Food: Seeds and suet from feeders; insects, grubs, and natural seeds on the ground; also berries and other fruit.

Nest: Nest boxes, in small holes in houses, barns and other outbuildings, or in pre-excavated holes in trees.

Rock pigeon

The bird with the iridescent throat and nape, gray wings and back is the original domestic pigeon; the other shades we see in city parks are the result of interbreeding with many other pigeon species.

Rock pigeon

Habitat: Cities, suburbs, and anywhere people congregate.

Food: "Feed the birds, tuppence a bag . . ." or bring your own seed or breadcrumbs, and pigeons will crowd around you in the middle of an intersection. These birds live entirely on what they scavenge from humans.

Nest: Nest boxes, in small holes in houses, barns and other outbuildings, or in pre-excavated holes in trees.

Mourning dove

With their gray-brown plumage and a series of dark gray spots on their wing coverts, mourning doves come in pairs or small flocks, frequenting the same feeders for months on end. Listen for the somber cooing that gives them their name—and also for the whistling sound their wings make as they take flight.

Habitat: Open lawns with sheltering woods or shrubs close by.

Food: Many kinds of seed.

Mourning dove

Nest: A tangle of loose twigs mashed flat, well above the ground in trees. Both male and female birds incubate the eggs, which hatch in thirteen to fourteen days.

Common grackle

Glossy purple-black with an iridescent blue head, the common is the smallest North American grackle. It's easy to spot this bird in flight, with its rudder-shaped tail creating a distinctive silhouette.

Habitat: Left to their own devices, grackles prefer open grassland, meadows, and marshes. Highly adaptable to human development, these birds now thrive in city and suburban neighborhoods.

Food: Grackles are notorious for stealing corn and other grains from farmers' fields. They do well with sunflower seed and berries from your shrubs, but they will forage through your trash given the opportunity.

Common grackle

Nest: High up in a pine or other conifer, often with easy access to water and open land for foraging. Eggs hatch in eleven to fifteen days.

White-crowned sparrow

Bright black and white head stripes make these little birds stand out in a flock of ground-feeding sparrows. Note the

White-crowned sparrow

long tail and clear, unmarked breast. First-year sparrows have buff-colored stripes instead of white.

Habitat: Forest and habitat edges with brushy shrubs; they forage at the boundaries of meadows and under feeders.

Food: Seeds and insects they find by scratching on the ground.

Nest: Cup-shaped nests are built in shrubs, from 1½ to 10 feet from the ground. Incubation is ten to fourteen days.

White-throated sparrow

The slow, plaintive, "Oh Sam Peabody-Peabody-Peabody" call announces this sparrow's arrival. Watch for a bird with a black-and-white striped head, bright yellow spots at the base of the bill, and a white throat.

White-throated sparrow

Habitat: Normally these birds prefer forests, where they rustle through leaves on the ground for food. In migration, they drop into backyards and feed along field and forest edges.

Food: Natural seeds and fruits, supplemented with black oil sunflower seeds from feeders.

Nest: On the ground in an existing depression, surrounded by dense vegetation. Incubation lasts twelve to fourteen days.

Brown-headed cowbird

The male's shiny, iridescent blue-black body creates a distinctive contrast with the dull brown head. The female is entirely slate gray with some subtle wing markings.

Habitat: Stands of trees, open areas on the edges of forests.

Brown-headed cowbird

Food: Seeds and insects found on the ground; cowbirds will come in flocks to graze through a lawn.

Nest: Cowbirds do not build nests. As parasitic breeders, they lay their eggs in other birds' nests and leave the young for the other species to raise.

Dark-eyed junco

With plumage variations by region, this little dark bird is the most reported feeder bird in America. Eastern "slate-colored" birds are dark gray with a pink bill and white underbelly.

Dark-eyed junco

Habitat: Open woods with clearings or areas of bare ground.

Food: Seeds and insects found on the ground; these birds are frequent feeder visitors in winter.

Nest: Often on the ground, hidden by grasses, weeds, and low shrub branches. Eggs hatch in twelve to thirteen days.

Indigo bunting

Usually found in open fields, this brilliant bunting may appear in yards in rural or sparsely developed areas. Its small, light-colored bill and solid royal blue coloring make it easy to identify. Look for the drab brown female bird nearby.

Indigo bunting

Habitat: Fields and farmland with little human activity, hedgerows, and brushy roadsides.

Food: Almost exclusively insects, with berries and seed when the bugs are scarce.

Nest: Close to the ground in a shrub or thick, leafy plant. Incubation takes twelve to thirteen days.

Wild turkey

There's no chance that you'll mistake this bird for anything else. Females are fairly uniformly brown with white-tipped feathers, while males feature extraordinary blue heads and red wattles when displaying.

Habitat: Normally open fields; more recently, turkeys wander into backyards in rural, suburban, and even urban areas.

Wild turkey

Food: Turkeys are omnivores, eating nuts, fruits, seeds, new spring buds, and the occasional amphibian.

Nest: On the ground, usually in an existing depression. It may take as long as twenty-six to twenty-eight days to incubate the eggs.

Northern bobwhite

Round and rust-colored, these secretive birds run from place to place. The white stripe above the eye and whitish throat can help you spot this bird, but the "Bob-WHITE" call is a bigger help in finding their location.

Habitat: Open tall grassland or woodlands, and marshes with tall vegetation.

Food: A plant eater, the bobwhite will occasionally visit a feeder and feed underneath it, usually returning to the same one for a season.

Nest: On the ground, often with a woven hood of grasses to conceal it. Incubation takes about twenty-four days.

Northern bobwhite

A gray squirrel hangs from a branch to reach a seed bell meant for birds.

11 Uninvited Backyard Guests

Backyard birding can be joyous as colorful, musical little birds frequent your feeders and bring their young to your trees and shrubs.

As you create your bird paradise, however, it's important to realize that nature will take its course right in your backyard—and that course is not always benevolent.

PREDATORS

Bird feeders present easy hunting for hawks and owls, predators that soar over your neighborhood looking for small animals to catch and kill for dinner. These larger birds have every right to eat, just as your feeder birds do, but they may exercise that right in your backyard when your back is turned . . . or even when it's not.

Several hawk species rank high among birds that come to feeders, according to the citizen science program Project FeederWatch. Cooper's,

Red-tailed hawk

sharp-shinned, and red-tailed hawks are among the most common birds of prey in the United States.

If you live in an open area with surrounding fields, watch at dusk for owls—large birds gliding swiftly over meadows and pastures, looking for rodents and small birds they can catch. Wooded areas also may attract owls, providing high perches from which they can watch for movements below that signal likely prey.

Most backyards do not attract hawks or owls, so the treacherous side of bird feeding may not visit your home. If hawks do avail themselves of your unintentional offerings, however, there's only one way to rid your yard of these hunters: Stop feeding the birds altogether.

The good news is that your birds generally know when a hawk is nearby. When all the birds in your yard suddenly dash for cover behind leaves or thorns, it's time to look up to see what kind of hawk is circling overhead.

You may observe the occasional *Wild Kingdom* moment, but these are your chances to marvel at the agility and skill with which large birds of prey acquire their targets.

NUISANCE BIRDS

Who invited the pigeons?

You did, when you put out seed for the white-crowned sparrows, mourning doves, and juncos you hoped to attract.

Pigeons, starlings, and house sparrows—three invasive species that are not native to the United States—and even crows can be facts of life for people who feed birds, particularly if you live in an urban or highly populated

House sparrows are now the most populous birds in the United States.

suburban area. All of these birds owe their livelihood to human development, and to their own ability to adapt. When natural food sources dwindled, these birds learned to eat what they could scavenge from humans. When trees fell in the path of progress, they began nesting in man-made nooks, on rooftops, and in whatever cozy cavities they could usurp from other birds.

Consequently it's inevitable that house sparrows, starlings, the occasional crows, and rock pigeons will find their way to your feeders. Worse, they may move in for good, taking up residence in or near your yard to have ready access to all of the good food you supply.

As these birds tend to arrive in flocks and tenaciously overstay their welcome, you may find yourself spending lots of money on seed to feed birds you don't want around.

What to do? If you don't want to stop feeding altogether, change the food you offer and the positions in which birds can eat it. Here are some strategies that work.

No falling seed

- Remove any ground-feeding options to discourage pigeons, crows, and starlings.
- Hang catchall plastic or net trays under your tube feeders to keep seed from falling to the ground. These trays sway when a large bird lands, so pigeons and crows won't try to perch on them.
- Starlings may still partake, but they will find less on the ground to satisfy their hunger.

Change your seed

- All feeder birds like black oil sunflower seed, but house sparrows, starlings, and grackles have trouble cracking open black stripe sunflower seeds. Switch to black stripe instead of black oil to fend off these birds.
- Grackles and starlings also dislike safflower seed. Small birds like chickadees and titmice eat it up.
- Don't offer cracked corn, a favorite of house sparrows, crows, and starlings.
- White millet and canary seed attract house sparrows, grackles, starlings, and cowbirds. Avoid seed blends that contain them.

The loop that works

- We were surprised to discover that this simple wire halo, hung just above a tube feeder, turned out to be very effective in warding off house sparrows. This magical method is the result of research conducted by the School of Natural Resources at the University of Nebraska, through which scientists discovered that house sparrows would not cross or fly under this wire hoop. Eventually the sparrows decide the halo is not threatening and return to the feeder, but it may take a year or more before they adjust.

Magic halo

- Others have found that hanging wire over platform feeders and even bluebird nest boxes deters sparrows as well.

Discourage nesting

- House sparrows and starlings will take over nest boxes intended for other species, especially bluebirds. They also nest in unwanted places—in the letters of hanging signs, or in drain pipes or gutters.
- As introduced, invasive species, house sparrows and European starlings are not protected by federal laws.

You are within your rights to evict these birds from whatever cavity they invade on your property.

- Keep an eye open for house sparrow and starling nesting activity, and remove the nesting material as soon as possible, before the birds incubate their eggs. This will discourage the birds.

THE NEIGHBOR'S CAT

One of the most insidious intruders in your backyard masquerades as a beloved pet.

Indoor cats can sit for hours watching feeders—a sort of reality TV show for your kitty. Outdoor cats can't resist the instinct that presses them to attempt to catch ground-feeding and perch-sitting birds.

If you own a cat, chances are good that you've already taken steps to keep it away from your backyard birds. What can you do, however, when the neighbor's cat wanders into your backyard and starts stalking its feathery prey?

It's an old-fashioned method, but a bell still works in alerting birds that a cat is approaching.

Start by checking the law in your community, to see if there's already legislation regarding wandering cats. Your neighbor may not be aware that the law requires the cat to be leashed or kept indoors. If the law is in your favor, call your local municipal Animal Control office, and let them deal with your neighbor.

If no law prevents the cat from spending its days outside, have a conversation with the cat's owner—perhaps while carrying the cat back to his or her home. Explain that you have created a bird garden in your yard for the purpose of attracting beautiful creatures, and that the roaming cat is taking too close an interest in the visitors at your feeders.

Your neighbor may be very resistant to keeping the cat indoors, particularly if the cat is accustomed to wandering at will. If this is the case, it's time to take the matter gently into your own hands. Try a motion-activated lawn sprinkler, which will turn on and spray the cat when it enters your yard. The spray lasts only a few seconds, but a couple of good soakings should be enough to annoy the cat into avoiding your property. You can find this device in your favorite home improvement store's garden section.

Meanwhile, protect your birds from the cat's advances by putting a bell on the cat's collar as a warning for the birds. It won't take long for birds to associate the tinkling bell with the cat. They will hear the sound and fly for safe perches in trees, on wires, and deep in shrubs. If your neighbor insists on allowing the cat to roam free, offer a bell as a compromise position—and offer to purchase it yourself.

Another method is to place feeders 10 to 12 feet from the nearest tree or shrub; this will bring birds close enough to cover to flee when necessary. Meanwhile, they will have a clear view of the surrounding yard, so they can spot the cat approaching. Don't place the feeders too far from cover, or the birds will not be able to escape into the trees if the cat pounces. Try shrubs like roses and hawthorns that offer thorns, an added level of protection. If a bird dives into a thorny bush when a cat approaches, it will only take one try before the cat learns not to reach into that bush again. Rose and hawthorn offer the added benefits of rose hips and berries in late summer, two treats for fruit-eating birds.

UNINVITED CRITTERS

With so much bird activity in your yard, you can be certain that you will attract additional visitors from your local animal kingdom.

The seed in your feeders and on the ground may attract some small animals, including squirrels, chipmunks, and mice. In winter months, your local deer may approach your feeders, especially toward the end of the season when other food sources have been exhausted. Deer populations across the country have expanded dramatically in recent years, as natural predators like wolves and bears have been extirpated from many areas. Parks and wildlife refuges often do not have enough natural food to sustain so many animals.

This eastern chipmunk figured out how to trick a squirrel-proof feeder.

Urban dwellers find themselves taken by surprise when raccoons, traditionally a woodland species, turn up in their backyards. Generally, these nocturnal creatures are more interested in the contents of your trash receptacles than in your feeders. They may be attracted to your yard by the bustling activity at your feeders, however, so you may see increased raccoon activity when you begin feeding birds in earnest.

You may think of coyotes as a species of the western deserts, but these wide-ranging, dog-like animals can now be found throughout North America. Coyotes have adapted well to urban sprawl, breeding in parks in metropolitan areas and foraging in suburban Dumpsters for food. They, too, find your garbage more interesting than your feeders, but birds that feed and nest on the ground are ready prey for these carnivores.

FOILING SQUIRRELS

It may take a few days or even weeks for birds to find your newly hung feeders . . . but squirrels will find them in a matter of hours.

Gray or red, flying or land-bound, squirrels are among the cleverest critters in the animal kingdom when it comes to finding new food sources. Highly motivated by seemingly inexhaustible appetites, these furry, broad-tailed creatures work tirelessly to find ways to beat the birds to your feeders. If you're feeding more seed and suet to squirrels than to your birds, you're not alone—virtually every bird gardener faces the squirrel dilemma.

Squirrels' remarkable flexibility, their ability to hang upside down by their back feet while feeding, and their

This feeder with a spinning bottom is one of the most popular squirrel deterrent feeders in the United States.

amazing prowess in leaping from trees to feeders—and not getting hurt if they miss and hit the ground—all contribute to their success. All of these skills also prevent us from foiling them for long.

To compound the problem, squirrels can climb smooth objects like poles, balance on a wire or other slim avenue, and keep their footing on slick surfaces. If they were not such nuisances at our bird feeding stations, we might be forced to admire and revere these talented animals.

That's why many manufacturers have invested large amounts of time and money in research and development, just to help bird gardeners keep the squirrels out of their birds' food. The result is a parade of products that can turn your squirrel problem into a source of endless amusement.

FEEDERS THAT WORK

Spend an afternoon watching how your squirrels gain access to your feeders. Do they jump up from a spot below the feeder? Do they walk the edge of your neighbor's fence and hop over to a feeder nearby? Or do they climb up through a shrub that's close to the feeder? The more you know about the access path, the more likely it is you can solve the problem, often without any outlay of funds. Here are feeder options that will work if you are looking to foil your neighborhood squirrels. We've tried many of these solutions, and some of them do indeed do the job.

Trick feeders

Trick feeders come in all shapes and sizes and in all price ranges. A popular option is a feeder with a spinning bottom that sends the squirrel flying when he applies his weight to the perch. Most birding specialty stores carry this feeder, which has a built-in rechargeable battery. No outdoor cord is required, but you will need to charge the battery every so often. Once the squirrels learn that they can't get to the food, they will back off.

Another option is a feeder with spring-loaded perches. This trick feeder (shown here) can hold the weight of small birds. When a squirrel puts its

Spring-loaded perches

weight on the perch, however, it gives way and the squirrel slips to the ground. Squirrels learn quickly, so once they've determined the seed is out of reach, they will lose interest.

Weight-activated feeders

A weight-activated feeder holds nearly ten pounds of seeds, but its perch balances delicately as if it were part of an old-fashioned scale. When more than two small birds land on the perch, it rocks down and closes off the seed dispenser openings. Squirrels will try for days to find a way in, but the rugged construction and sensitive perch mechanism keep them from accessing any of the seed. Be sure to place this feeder a good distance from branches or other feeders, so the squirrel can't keep its weight on another perch while trying to get past this one.

A second option is a little mesh feeder, a perfect addition to a small garden, which has a built-in spring that responds to weight. Two or three birds can use the perches and feast on the seed inside, but squirrels are too heavy. When they try to climb on, the mesh lowers and shuts off the feeder's holes. Squirrels can't even climb on top and reach down the feeder, as this will close the feeder holes.

Squirrel cage

Here's a caged feeder that lets woodpeckers, nuthatches, sparrows, and other birds in, but keeps squirrels out. The suet stays in the center of the cage, allowing birds to enter the cage, perch comfortably and eat the suet in peace. The cage's mesh is too small to allow a squirrel to enter, or even reach in through the bars.

A suet feeder with a squirrel cage lets woodpeckers in, but keeps squirrels out.

Roller feeder

This ingenious device is weighted to keep its roof upright, providing a sloping surface for the squirrels. Squirrels can handle a tilted footing, but once they put their weight on this feeder, it rolls—sending the squirrel sprawling. As it rolls, it closes the feeding holes, so even the most determined squirrels can't get in.

Roller feeder

Squirrel feeders

It seems like a good idea on the surface: Give the squirrels their own food, and maybe they'll leave the birds' food alone.

If only it were that simple!

Squirrels will indeed rush readily to the feeder you offer them, whether it's full of peanuts in the shell or it holds an upright, bright yellow cob of corn.

The problem, however, is that squirrels have no sense of "mine" and "theirs." They will spend some time distracted from their job of finding a way to your bird feeders, gobbling down the nuts or corn cob. Once these food sources have been exhausted, however, they will be back at the bird feeders with renewed energy and vigor.

So should we skip the squirrel feeders? One of the advantages of these devices is that they may be the only feeders in your yard that are not at the end of an obstacle course of challenges. If you're already using squirrel-proof feeders, your squirrels probably know that they can't penetrate these—but it may not stop them from trying.

Distracting the squirrels with choice morsels of their own can buy you some squirrel-less time at your other feeders. Industrious squirrels will stop interfering with birds' feeding habits, at least for short bursts of time.

Placing a platform or dish feeder on the ground with squirrel treats in it—dried whole-kernel corn and nuts— also will keep squirrels busy. When food is plentiful without much expense of effort, squirrels will take the path of least resistance, leaving your seed feeders alone while they devour whatever is easiest to get.

ALTERNATIVES THAT WORK (OR DON'T)

Despite your best efforts and the most innovative squirrel-proof feeders on the market, your squirrels may still find a way into your sunflower seed–stocked hopper and tube feeders.

Baffles

All is not yet lost! Try some of the baffles that cut off a squirrel's access to the feeders before the animal gets close.

Small hanging baffle on a tube feeder

Some baffles work on the same weight-activated principles as squirrel-resistant feeders do, but others create a tunnel or compartment that stops the squirrel in its tracks. None of these devices hurt the squirrels in any way, but they do frustrate the squirrels' efforts to reach your feeders' contents.

Your birding specialty store or home improvement store are well stocked with all kinds of baffles: tubular, flat, domed, and otherwise. There's a solution to fit any size feeder or space, and most are fairly inexpensive.

Choose baffles made from durable, teeth-resistant materials like steel, Plexiglas, and polycarbonate plastics. Squirrels will chew through anything they can to get to your seed, so look for materials that are impervious to this kind of punishment. The baffles you select should be easy to install, versatile enough to fit many different kinds of feeders, and—most important—the baffle should not block your view of the birds visiting your feeders.

DIY: CREATE YOUR OWN BAFFLE

Create your own baffles and deterrents out of materials you may have around the house:

- Wrap the feeder pole with metal flashing, which prevents squirrels from gaining a foothold as they climb.

- If your feeder hangs from a clothesline or other line across your yard, thread the chain or line through a series of plastic tubes, cans, or other cylinders from one end to the other. When the squirrel walks across on the way to the feeder, the tubes will spin, dumping the squirrel on the ground.

- Make your feeder pole out of PVC pipe. Squirrels can't get solid footing on PVC material.

Squirrel-blocking solutions

Defeating the wily squirrel has become a hobby of its own, a high-spirited struggle between humans and nature. The wide-ranging list of solutions involves various kinds of nontoxic chemicals, odor agents, alternate seed combinations, and even the old-fashioned catch-and-release—all of which provide the fun of watching squirrel behavior as they experience one product or process after another.

Manufacturers now offer many products at outdoor recreation, farm and feed, and garden stores, with an even more inspired selection online (search "squirrel deterrents"). Most bird gardeners try these products sequentially, seeing what works and using another solution to augment whatever success the first one offers.

How effective are all of these products? As in all fields of endeavor, some solutions may prove very effective, while others may have no discernable effect at all.

Chili peppers contain a natural chemical called capsaicin, which gives peppers their spicy heat. Squirrels appear to hate seed or suet coated with capsaicin—at least until they get used to it. Treated seed and suet are generally a little more expensive than food that does not contain the hot chemical. Birds in South America eat so many chili peppers that some species are called "bird peppers." It stands to reason that the birds will not be put off by capsaicin-treated food, although these products receive mixed reviews from backyard birders.

Other possible deterrents include a cloth bag or sock filled with mothballs, placed in the path to feeders; rags soaked with ammonia, placed near feeders; coyote urine (available in bottles); organic squirrel repellents, available at garden centers; cayenne pepper mixed into conventional birdseed, or a high frequency-emitting device that irritates squirrels (and other animals).

If you choose to engage in the eternal battle with squirrels, keep in mind that each deterrent you put in place may have an unintended impact on birds or other animals. Skip any kind of harsh chemicals, especially poisons, as rabbits, voles, chipmunks, and other small furry creatures may ingest these poisons. Pesticides have a significant negative impact on birds—in fact, many bird species lingered for decades on the nation's endangered species lists because of toxic chemicals in pesticides. While these dangerous substances are now banned from use by law, newer chemicals may not have a long enough track record to determine their effects. Stick with natural, non-toxic deterrents to keep your backyard safe for wildlife.

Wood is no good

Don't use wooden bird feeders! Squirrels chew through these in a matter of hours, emptying them of their seed. Instead, choose feeders made of hard plastic and/or metal, durable materials that resist squirrels' industrious teeth.

Don't build a pathway

Squirrels will find a highway to your feeders if you let them. Here are some situations to avoid:

- Keep trees trimmed back from feeders. Squirrels will run down the branches and leap onto the feeder.
- Look out for downspouts and wiring. Squirrels can scamper up a drainpipe or climb an electrical or cable wire to get to feeders close to your windows.
- Extend hanging hardware away from porch or deck railings, so the squirrel can't jump from the railing to the feeder.

APPENDIX A:
SEASONAL BIRDING CHECKLISTS

Spring checklist
Feeders and seed

❑ Take all of your feeders down and clean them thoroughly. Disinfect with a weak solution of one part household bleach to ten parts water.

❑ Get your hummingbird and oriole feeders out: early April for Connecticut and Rhode Island, and early May in Massachusetts, Vermont, New Hampshire, and Maine.

❑ Discard any remaining butcher suet as soon as daily temperatures rise above 40 degrees. Switch to packaged "all season" or "no melt" suet blends.

❑ Get out your mealworm feeder, and add mealworms to attract bluebirds. Use live mealworms until the weather gets too hot for them.

Birdbaths and ponds

❑ Remove water defrosters from your birdbaths. Clean and store them for next winter.

❑ Clean your birdbaths and refill them.

❑ Do a "wet run" of your water circulators (pumps) to make sure they're functioning properly. Check all electrical connections, and repair or replace if necessary.

❑ Skim winter detritus off of the surface of your pond. Add barley or other algae inhibitor.

Nest boxes

❑ Check all your nesting boxes for signs that birds roosted in them over the winter.

❑ If the boxes have been used, scrape out and clean them before birds begin nesting.

❑ Put out nesting material in suet cages or seed wreaths, or on its own.

Garden

- ❑ It's finally time to snip last year's blossoms from your perennials.

- ❑ Pick or prune off any remaining berries from last year's crop, and discard.

- ❑ Rake any twigs or branches that fell over the winter into your brush pile.

- ❑ Rake up and discard the winter's seed shells and rejected seed under your feeders.

- ❑ Pull any new shoots under your feeders that may be sprouting from last year's birdseed. Watch for possible sunflower sprouts, and transplant them to your perennial garden.

- ❑ Plan where you'd like to add annuals, new perennials, shrubs, or trees. Make a list to take to garden centers.

- ❑ Have fun planting!

Summer checklist

Feeders and seed

- ❑ As weather warms, change the nectar in your hummingbird feeders every three days.

- ❑ Change the orange halves on your oriole feeder every few days as well, to keep oranges from generating mold.

- ❑ After heavy rains or in very humid weather, change the seed in your feeders to keep it from becoming moldy.

- ❑ Watch underneath your seed feeders for shell build-up. Rake seed and shells onto a shovel or dustpan and discard.

- ❑ Clean and disinfect feeders as needed.

- ❑ Watch your deck, railings, and squirrel baffles for bird droppings. Clean away this material as soon as possible.

Birdbaths and ponds

❏ Change the water in your birdbaths daily throughout the summer.

❏ Maintain the level of algae deterrent in your pond.

❏ Add a mister to your bird bath to cool birds in the heat.

Nest boxes

❏ Watch for nesting, feeding and fledging activity.

❏ When birds have abandoned a nest after fledglings have flown, clean out the nest box. Remove the old nest and discard it.

❏ Keep an eye out for house sparrow nests in inconvenient places on your property. Remove and discard nests if you wish.

❏ Remember that no matter where they are located, it's illegal to disturb active nests of birds that are native to the United States.

Garden

❏ Leave dead flowers in place on seed-producing perennials (sunflower, coneflower, black-eyed Susan, and many others).

❏ Resist the urge to use pesticides—let the birds clear out your bugs.

❏ Monitor under your feeders for unwanted sprouts from germinating bird seed. Remove them as they appear.

Fall checklist

Feeders and seed

❏ In the northern states and provinces, leave hummingbird and oriole feeders out until mid-October for migrating stragglers.

- [ ] Bring out your high-capacity seed feeders. Fill them with sunflower and safflower seed to give birds extra energy during migration.

- [ ] Place your ground-level platform feeders, and add millet for migrating or arriving juncos, winter sparrows, and siskins.

- [ ] When temperatures regularly rise only into the 40s, put out your butcher suet.

Birdbaths and ponds

- [ ] Place your birdbath defroster in your birdbath when the first frost is predicted.

- [ ] Shut off water circulators when temperatures are predicted to drop below freezing.

Nest boxes

- [ ] Clean out the last nests of the season.

- [ ] Scrape and wash out your nest boxes.

- [ ] Leave the boxes in place to provide shelter for roosting birds in winter.

Garden

- [ ] Leave dead blossoms in place on seed-producing perennials, to feed birds throughout the migration and winter.

- [ ] Rake fall leaves. Compost or recycle most of this, but leave some under shrubs to provide shelter to overwintering birds.

- [ ] Prune dead branches and twigs from your shrubs. Add these to your brush pile.

- [ ] Leave as many berries in place as possible. Birds will return in winter to eat the fermented fruit.

Winter checklist

Feeders and seed

- ❏ Take in your hummingbird and oriole feeders. Clean these and store them until spring.

- ❏ Keep your seed feeders filled for overwintering birds.

- ❏ If you don't usually feed with nuts, add a peanut feeder in winter.

- ❏ Replenish suet often.

- ❏ Rub some suet on the bark of your largest trees for brown creepers, woodpeckers, and nuthatches.

Birdbaths and ponds

- ❏ Check your birdbath defrosters regularly to be sure the GFI has not shut them off. Reset and find the issue if necessary.

- ❏ Maintain open water in your birdbaths as much as possible during the coldest weather.

Nest boxes

- ❏ Place some wood shavings in your clean nest boxes to provide warmth for roosting birds.

- ❏ Add a roosting box (hole in the bottom) if you wish. These boxes provide perches inside for birds, and are usually larger to accommodate small flocks.

Garden

- ❏ Leave dead blossoms to allow birds to eat the seeds.

- ❏ Begin planning your spring garden goals. This is a great time of year to get catalogs, review websites, and make a list of the new plants, shrubs, and trees you will add when the weather warms.

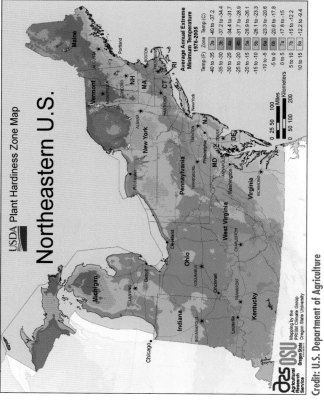

Credit: U.S. Department of Agriculture

Index

About the Author and Photographer

Randi and Nic Minetor crisscross the region regularly to research and shoot photos for their books on birds, hiking, history and America's national parks. A husband and wife team, they have worked together on eighteen books to date, including *Backyard Birding: A Guide to Attracting and Identifying Birds, Hiking Waterfalls in New York, Scenic Routes & Byways New York,* and *Hiking Through History New York,* as well as five FalconGuides *National Park Pocket Guides* to Great Smoky Mountains, Acadia, Zion and Bryce Canyon, and Everglades National Parks, and Gulf Islands National Seashore. Their work also includes Globe Pequot Press's *Historical Tours* series, with four books completed: *Washington, DC, Gettysburg, Fredericksburg,* and *New York Immigrant Experience.* Randi wrote five books in FalconGuides' *Best Easy Day Hikes* series, for Rochester, Buffalo, Syracuse, Albany, and the Hudson River Valley, for which Nic provided cover and website photos. Randi is also the author of *Day Trips: Hudson Valley* and *Cursed in New York: Stories of the Damned in the Empire State.*

When not on the road, Nic is the lighting designer for Eastman Opera Theatre, theatrical productions at the National Technical Institute for the Deaf, and Finger Lakes Opera, as well as lighting director for the PBS series *Second Opinion.* Randi owns a writing and public relations firm serving corporate and non-profit clients. The Minetors live in Rochester, NY.